NEW LIGHT ON LONGFELLOW

H.W.L. "in the clouds"
at Göttingen!

LONGFELLOW AS A STUDENT AT GÖTTINGEN
Drawn by himself

NEW LIGHT ON LONGFELLOW

BY
JAMES TAFT HATFIELD

GORDIAN PRESS
NEW YORK
1970

Originally Published 1933
Reprinted 1970

Library of Congress Catalog Card Number — 70-114097
SBN   87752-050-X
Published by GORDIAN PRESS, INC.

PREFACE

THIS book was begun as a special study of Longfellow's relations to Germany, a study which had been called for, and which seems to be justified, particularly in view of various immature utterances which have been made upon the subject. Respectable scholars have published valuable treatises, drawn, almost without exception, from the copious materials contained in Samuel Longfellow's *Life of Henry Wadsworth Longfellow.* This is one of the best of biographies, a quarry from which many learned works have been hewn; but it implies no disparagement of Samuel Longfellow's excellent work when one points out that its author was inadequately versed in German literary subjects, and omitted much important matter concerning them.

The present offering, which has gone somewhat beyond its original plan, is chiefly based upon a conscientious investigation of the mountainous mass of unpublished sources preserved in Craigie House — diaries, correspondence, lecture-notes, first drafts of works, scrapbooks, albums, and the like — to which the most liberal access was granted.

Chapter XI attempts an estimate of Longfellow's entire life and writings. Beginning this book with a fairly open mind, though with a general impression that Longfellow's writings represented an *überwundener Standpunkt*, the author has come to know him thoroughly, from a minute study of the most intimate documents of his life: the result has been a gradual and complete conversion to the belief that our poet is one toward whom every honest American may cherish the highest pride and affection — without reservations or apologies.

[v]

PREFACE

Gratitude is expressed to the descendants of the poet, Mrs. Joseph G. Thorp and Mr. H. W. L. Dana, who, with that public-spirited generosity which has characterized the family, have opened every door of opportunity, and have given invaluable advice and information. Professor Edward Everett Hale has furnished items from the unpublished diary of his distinguished father. To Mrs. Edward MacDowell, director of the MacDowell Colony, who has offered ideal conditions for creative work, to the MacDowell Society of Evanston, Illinois, and to Northwestern University must also be given thanks for their liberal help in bringing this work to an end.

J. T. H.

NORTHWESTERN UNIVERSITY

CONTENTS

ILLUSTRATIONS

NEW LIGHT ON LONGFELLOW

.:

CHAPTER I

Earlier Days

By being born into the high New England tradition, in the
favored city of Portland, Longfellow became a representa-
tive of the sweet reasonableness, the sense of order and
proportion, which made that civilization essentially Greek
in spirit — in spite of very obvious differences between
Puritan New England and the Attica of Pericles.

Daily life was surrounded by dignified self-respect and
decorous neatness, to which was added a distinct note of
stateliness. Typical homes were spacious, beautifully pro-
portioned, neatly painted, and set among well-kept grounds
and gay gardens; careful thrift forbade waste or vulgar
luxury.

With a general capitulation to speed, noise, size, and glare
in these United States, the older American tradition has
suffered no slight attenuation — traces of survival being,
perhaps, most readily discoverable in certain parts of the
Vermont or New Hampshire of our time.

Both of the boy's parents represented this stock in full
purity, as regards descent and personal character. High-
mindedness, cultivated tastes, a proud instinct for cleanli-
ness, a fixed devotion to immaterial values — these things
determined the spirit of the home, and insured that the
gifted son should be given careful training, from his earliest
days. A fastidious aversion from swinishness, in any of its

[1]

manifestations, went with him through life. After making farewell calls on leaving Heidelberg, he wrote in his diary: 'One nasty little Professor in a dirty *Schlafrock...* took his pipe out of his mouth and kissed me on the lips! I had a great mind to shake him by the ears. I had as lief kiss a pig.'

Apart from regular schooling, a certain Nolcini, who taught Italian, music, and dancing in Portland, was engaged to tutor the boy in French, and seems to have brought him to the point of being able to carry on correspondence in that language. A little later, a German, living in Portland, carried on the private instruction in French. Music was favored, and young Henry became a good player upon the flute. Books were abundant in the home, and were not only eagerly read, but assimilated — beginning with very tender years.

Longfellow's father (a graduate of Harvard) stood very high in the respect of the public, and carried many heavy responsibilities throughout his honored life. Serious, sane, public-spirited, he bore heroically an increasing burden of illness and suffering during twenty-eight years; long after this was known to be fatal, and while subject to harrowing attacks, he kept up his legal duties in the courts. A man of clearly pronounced convictions, but open to reason. Through life, he was the friend and sympathetic adviser of his son, whose personality he respected, even when disagreeing with his decisions. 'My ambition,' he wrote, while his son was a student at Bowdoin, 'has never been to accumulate wealth for my children, but to cultivate their minds in the best possible manner, and to imbue them with correct moral, political, and religious principles.'

A certain note of rigid pedantry cannot be gainsaid: he objected to the boy's verse, 'Beneath the dark and motionless beech,' because of its 'irregularity'; he condemned the title *Outre-Mer* (perhaps the best feature of that immature work), and proposed: 'Sketches of France, Spain, and Italy by an American.' When Longfellow was elected to the Smith Professorship at Harvard, it was self-evident that he must enrich the very sketchy knowledge of German which he had caught up during his first stay in Europe — but his father wrote: 'With respect to the idea of going again to Europe, *we all think you must not indulge it, or give any reason to expect it.* Mary [Longfellow's girl wife] is delighted with the prospect of Change, but not with the idea of going to Europe.' He was equally gloomy about the son's third (and supremely remunerative) visit to Germany, though the young professor had just paid all the debts incurred during the second trip. The same 'safe-and-sane' attitude appears in his frequent admonitions against sacrificing college interests to literary work: 'You should devote no more time to these subjects, than you have *leisure,* after the performance of your Official duties, and *this* with *due regard to your health.*'

With humanistic tastes, the father shared the classical interests of his son as a college student, and later took high pride in his literary work: 'I have not been able to turn to your Books [*Hyperion* and *Voices of the Night*] without tears of joy.'

It was natural that he should be deeply concerned with the upholding of the proud Puritan tradition, and thus he writes to his son, who was living at the time in Rome: 'Persevere, my dear Son, in all your good resolutions, and return to us with all your virtues heightened and invigorated, and your mind strengthened, cultivated, and improved, prepared for great usefulness and respectability.' (Incidentally, this is what happened — a result which our day finds it so impossible to forgive.)

[3]

Longfellow's mother, Zilpah, was a sweet, fine, intellectual lady, quite able to discuss stimulating literary problems with her student son, a thoughtful counselor as to their values. She took equal part with the Father in considering his plans in Europe. She gave him sound advice to keep clear of 'those who use the American French, as your fellow-boarders must do.' She was terror-stricken at the thought of his studying in Göttingen, among licentious, dueling students. Fortunately, he went — in the face of her repeated protests. The long, affectionate correspondence between mother and son, continuing until her death in 1851, makes delightful reading.

At the age of fourteen, the boy was registered as Freshman in Bowdoin College, but did the first year's work in the Portland home. The curriculum was 'set,' but solid and fairly comprehensive: Latin, Greek, mathematics, chemistry, anatomy and philosophy were faithfully covered. He wrote to his mother, 'I am naturally indolent' — but his college record shows no trace of his having yielded to such a tendency. He read widely in serious French literature, driven, apparently, by his own interest, and he was generally known as the widest and most critical reader in an unusually gifted class, which included John S. C. Abbott and Nathaniel Hawthorne. An independent spirit crops out in his active efforts to establish a Unitarian society in the very precincts of orthodox Bowdoin.

While still a Junior, he had firmly resolved to devote his whole life to literature, and his early offerings in prose and verse found a cordial welcome from the *American Monthly Magazine* in Philadelphia, and the *United States Literary Gazette* in Boston; the latter journal published seventeen of his poems during his Senior year: his writings already began to attract attention in literary circles. Only a few of these poems (which disclose the direct influence of Bryant) were republished in Longfellow's first volume. They show a mild pensiveness in the contemplation of nature; several of them have to do with the American Indian. A longing for the South and for foreign parts is evident: *Italian Scenery* is a sort of comprehensive Baedeker of that alluring country — compiled among the forests of Maine.

As college life drew to its close, there were searching discussions between father and son as to the career that should follow. The line of least resistance was plainly that of entering the legal profession, but the youth had made his choice. He had seriously considered West Point, or the life of a farmer, but his purpose became fixed on future eminence in literature: 'My whole soul burns most ardently for it, and every earthly thought centres in it,' he writes to his father early in the Senior year. He would waste no time in mastering any other bread-winning profession. 'Surely there never was a better opportunity offered for the exertion of literary talent in our own country.' As an immediate plan he proposed to his father, who assented, that he should spend a year at Harvard, immersing himself in the study of general literature, and, at the same time, 'gaining as perfect a knowledge of the French and Italian languages as can be gained by study.' If literature offered no prospects, at the end of this time, he was prepared to take up the law.

When he was graduated, at the age of eighteen (being fourth in his class), he gave a prophetic oration (reminding one of young Klopstock at Schulpforta, outlining the plan for a future German religious epic), in which he scored the want of undivided attention to letters in America, to 'the utter abandonment of everything else,' and defended the glory of literature as an exclusive calling.

But just at this Commencement-time, the Trustees of

Bowdoin voted to establish a new chair of Modern Languages. To young Longfellow, whose finished ability in the ancient classics had attracted attention, this appointment was tendered informally, with the proposal that he repair to Europe (without expense to the college), to fit himself for his new duties. He was only too willing to accept this offer as a help to his life-plan; his father, always generous where an investment could be made for the future of his children, promised the necessary support, allowing fifteen hundred dollars for the purpose.[1] The young man busied himself with writing at home until the end of April, 1826, when he left to take passage from New York to Havre. On May 2, he dined with George Ticknor in Boston: this date has a significance with which we shall be increasingly concerned, for it marks the poet's first connection with Germany and German studies.[2] Ticknor 'strongly recommended a year's residence in Germany,' and was 'very decidedly in favor of commencing literary studies there.' The historian of Spanish literature enjoyed great prestige on the Continent, and gave the younger man valuable letters of introduction.

In passing through Northampton, a call was made at the celebrated Round Hill School, conducted by Joseph Cogswell and George Bancroft, both of whom recommended a year's residence in Göttingen — where Ticknor and Bancroft had studied. The son wrote back to his father:

> Ticknor says... that it is all-important to have a knowledge of the German language. The Lectures on literary history, which he wishes me to attend there, commence in October, and

[1] In 1850, he quite properly took the expenses of these three years into account, in reckoning with the family.

[2] Two years later, while her son was still in Europe, his mother wrote him that a friend had just called at the Portland home for 'german books,' and could be given only 'a collection of fables, and a grammar.' It would be interesting to learn how these books got there.

he says I could before that time become sufficiently advanced in the language to understand them. I should take rooms there as at Paris, and should pay about one guinea for a course of Lectures. It will, he thinks,... be laying a solid foundation for future literary requirements.

For my own part — I must confess that this change in my original plan did not strike me very favorably at first, but the more I reflect upon it the better I like it.

On May 15, 1826, he sailed for France — 'full of youth and hope and enthusiasm.'

CHAPTER II

The First European Trip

LANDING in France, and having had no answer from home to his inquiries about Göttingen, Longfellow proceeded at once to Paris, where he lived for morc than eight months. The present study is less concerned with this Romance period, which includes a subsequent eight months in Spain, and a full year in Italy. In the earlier stages, we must think of Longfellow as an eager boy, working tirelessly for a practical mastery of the Romance languages, and with the fixed policy of making his home with native families of the better sort. He struck his roots deep into popular soil, and was by no means *blöde* in making close contacts. From his (unpublished) journal of May, 1827, we learn of his joining so heartily in the village dance at Pardillo, that, with his hands whirling in the air, he knocked off the manager's hat. While living in this hamlet, he made friends with the surgeon, the curé, the village secretary, and took part in various rustic sports: 'I have seen a little of Spanish rural life, and am much delighted with it. I like to see things in reality — not in painting — to study men, not books:

> ... jucundum est, rerum radices scrutare — nam:
> Dulcius ex ipso fonte bibuntur aquae.' [1]

In Venice he made friends with the gondolier poet, Toni Toscan, who had served Lord Byron. At the other end of the social scale, he was securely at his ease in the salons of Paris (where he met Sidney Smith, Cooper, and M. Julian);

[1] MS. journal. A few years later, Ticknor gave his weighty testimony as to Longfellow's mastery of written and spoken Spanish.

[8]

in Florentine and Venetian society among Russians, French [1] and English; in Madrid and in Dresden. Mrs. Everett, wife of the American Ambassador to Spain, said, 'His countenance is itself a letter of recommendation'; and Lieutenant Slidell, who traveled with him in Spain, spoke of his 'sunny locks, fresh complexion, and a clear blue eye — all indications of a joyous temperament.' His intimate journals witness to the abandon with which he gave himself to the captivating spell of the South: 'There are moments in our lives, to which we feel that romance could add nothing — that poetry itself could not beautify!' Grenada 'carried his thoughts away from the realities of life to the musings of romance.' In the youthful home letters we cannot fail to notice that unfailing attention to style and expression which mark the consecrated literary artist.

Throughout this period, there are no traces of a special interest in German. At Montefiascone he does not detect the true name 'Johann Fugger' at the tomb of 'Jean Defoucris'; in Florence he copies into his diary, in faultless *Frakturschrift*, a rather shady, but distinctly witty, German quatrain.

For the greater part of three years, discussions with the powers at home were in progress as to the distribution of time, especially as to the importance of a long stay in Göttingen, as urged by Ticknor and Bancroft — a project in which the Family entertained a decidedly mild interest. On the day after landing in Havre, Longfellow wrote to his brother, inquiring whether his father had received his letter 'concerning going to Germany.' These diplomatic conversations were made the more complicated from the fact that letters took from two to four months to arrive. In August,

---

[1] Princess Charlotte, Bonaparte's cousin, and wife of his brother Charles, drew a portrait of the young traveler in her album, at Florence.

1826, his father suggested France, Spain, Italy, and Göttingen — 'if it should be thought advisable to visit that place'; he even suggested 'a number of months' there, after a 'few months' in Italy — but held the subject open for full discussion. In fact, this order was actually followed — though the proportions were much altered. In October the son wrote:

> I am convinced that if I remain here but two years, I had better relinquish the Spanish language for the German — since I cannot acquire a thorough knowledge of four languages in so short a time. This was the advice which Mr. Bancroft and Mr. Cogswell gave me.

He wishes to spend the summer and succeeding winter in Germany, 'inasmuch as the German language is infinitely more important than the Spanish, being infinitely more rich in literary resources.' In October he writes a spirited but respectful letter to his father, who had expected him to 'master' French in four or five months, and then proceed to Spain. However strong the romantic lure of that country (and the young man's later response to this was one of the happiest experiences of his life), he would rather give up Spain and Italy than leave the French half-acquired, and he is convinced that German is all-important.

> I do not imagine that I could learn to speak the German with correctness and fluency in the space of a year — but if I go there in the Spring instead of going into Italy, I shall learn the language perfectly enough to read it, and to understand the Literary lectures which commence in November.... I had rather be master of the German and French than to know them superficially together with the Italian and Spanish, and I make this proposition to you as the one which of all others I should choose.

Between German and Italian, he elects German. In a long letter, October 26, 1826, his solicitous mother warns him against Göttingen and its degrading influences; the acquisition of the language would keep him away beyond the time allotted [a year and a half], and she also fears a 'confusion of Babel' in the young man's mind, if he learns any more languages.

Longfellow's prompt answer was written from Paris:

I have never had any particular fondness for a duel.... It would be useless to go into Germany unless I could remain at least a year.... When I wrote my last letter upon the subject, speaking of my going to Göttingen as a matter almost certain, I thought I could learn the language and get some insight into the literature in a shorter time than a twelvemonth, but those who are best acquainted with the subject tell me no. The language is so exceedingly difficult that it will not be worth while to speak it unless I have much time to devote to it.

He accordingly resigns the prospect of Germany altogether. His father's letter on December 3 was more to the point:

The situation you have in view cannot be obtained unless you qualify yourself to teach both French and Spanish correctly.

In Stephen Longfellow's opinion, the relations between the United States and South America were rapidly increasing, so that the acquisition of Spanish was a *sine qua non*.[1]

I consider [continued his father] the knowledge of the Spanish of more importance to you than German and Italian.... I had supposed that six months in France and three or four months in Spain would be sufficient.... You will not probably be able to remain abroad more than two years.... I consider the German language and literature much more important than the Italian, and if you can learn only one, the former is to be preferred.

[1] This argument is not unfamiliar at the present time; Longfellow seems to have had very little to do with teaching Spanish at Harvard, in spite of his phenomenal command of the language.

To this the son replied:

> I cannot imagine who told you that six months was enough for
> the French — he would have been more correct if he had said
> six years.

And, from Madrid some months later,

> Do not believe too much of what people tell you of learning
> the French language in six months, and the Spanish in three.
> Were I guided by such counsellors I should return a sheer charla-
> tan; and though I might deceive others as to the amount of my
> knowledge, I cannot deceive myself so easily; for whatever
> vanity I may possess with regard to my natural abilities, I have
> very little with regard to my acquisitions.

In January, 1827, his father stresses the necessity of becoming well acquainted with French, Spanish, and German,
and offers to 'extend your time a little.'

The solicitous mother, however, did not abandon her
position so readily, but brought up reserves, by consulting
Mr. Justice Story, who had been a classmate of her husband
at Harvard, in the matter of the proposed year at Göttingen:

> He seemed to think the advantages would not compensate for
> the time and expence of spending another year abroad.... He
> thought you might get the German well enough in this country,
> for all useful purposes.... Judge S., you know, is a scholar, and a
> man of liberal views. I hope you will think as he does respecting
> Germany.... I do not believe the language, that is the pronuncia-
> tion of it, would ever be of much advantage to you here, you
> would never have an opportunity of conversing, and you would
> find very few indeed who would wish to learn it.

But Longfellow's father had been to a more competent
source of advice, and his letter of August 25, 1827, to his son
in Madrid, expresses handsomely his full conversion to the
German plan:

I have recently seen Mr. Ticknor, who appears very anxious that you should go to Germany. He says the acquisition of the German language will be of more importance to you as a literary man than any two other languages within his knowledge, as it unlocks a vast store of learning, and you find in that language the best treatises on French, Spanish, and even English literature that are to be found in any language.... I am disposed to do all in my power to make your education as perfect as possible, and as you are now abroad, should be sorry for you to omit any thing which would occasion regret hereafter.... As there is no gentleman in this State who is master of the German language, it is desirable that you should learn it, if you can do it, without too much time and expense.

Accordingly, at the end of the year, writing from Marseilles on his way to Italy, Longfellow proposed to make short work of Italian studies and to press on to 'Gottingen' early in the next year. Soon after, he asks his father's advice about the University of Bonn, recommended to him by Ambassador Everett, who had also given him letters to certain of its professors. A few days later, he wrote to his mother, from Florence, that he was

anxious to get into Germany; at least as much so as I am to see Rome and Naples.... I am travelling through Italy without any enthusiasm.... The fact is, I am homesick for Spain.

At the end of the year (all of which had been spent in Italy), he is leaving for Dresden, where he is determined to do all that can be done in a short time toward acquiring a competent knowledge of German. While in Vienna (January, 1829), he copied into his diary, in careful German script, five lines of the *Nachtwächterlied* ('*Hört, ihr Herren*'), after which he resumed his record in French. Being 'melancholy and down-hearted' a week later, he is now disposed to go on, as soon as possible, to find his college classmate, Ned Preble (son of the Commodore) at Göttingen — though he has a scruple that this would impede his progress in German: 'On reaching Dresden I shall be better able to judge.' Before the middle of January he reached this first city of his German academic residence, and made his quarters in Günther's inn, 'The Golden Crown.' Washington Irving, who had made many friends in Dresden in 1823,[1] had fortified the young man with letters of introduction, and he was welcomed into the vivid life of a highly cosmopolitan society: balls and tableaux, concerts and opera became rivals of his serious studies. On January 28, he was feeling 'very blue.' It is evident that he did not abandon his learned labors, for we have entries like: 'busy with studies all day'; 'den ganzen Tag zu Haus.' On one occasion he refused Baron von Löwenstein's invitation to dinner. Doubtless he 'did' some German, but it is apparent that his chief interest was still in the Romance field: in the Public Library, to which he was introduced by Hofrat Böttiger,[2] he works only on Spanish materials. He kept his private diary in French, and composed a prose sketch, *Un Bon Vivant*, in that language, dealing characteristically with the bourgeois frequenters of the 'Golden Crown.' From this may be translated a robust story told by a vagrant peddler:

A prince, who had just been married, made a tour through his territory, accompanied by his young wife. The well-disposed villagers, in a hamlet through which he passed, wished to do him honor, and outdid one another in making him gifts. Among others, the locksmiths had a painting made, with portraits of the prince and princess, and, at the bottom, a baby in a cradle, to show that the people hoped that this marriage might be blessed by the birth of a son and heir. Below it was the inscription: 'Die Schlosser haben Dieses gemacht!'

[1] PMLA, XLV, 1154.
[2] Böttiger, to whom L. brought a letter from Irving, had been closely associated with Goethe, Schiller, Herder and Wieland during his Weimar days.

As the young man explained to his father, he had found 'several inconveniences for a studious life' in Dresden, and he had a strong desire to see his old friend Preble, into whose welcoming arms he accordingly rushed, reaching Göttingen on the twenty-second of February, 1829.[1] The wholesome effect of this full companionship is reflected in the documents of their common life. After Longfellow's arrival, Preble gave up his quarters, and they were settled on the Weenderstrasse, just opposite the ancient town hall. They kept house, breakfasted and dined together, and attended the same lectures. The joy of the first meeting is expressed in the account sent to Portland:

OLD FRIENDS [2]

I cannot describe the sensations which filled my breast when my postillion reined up at the gate of Göttingen, and looking into the post-chaise asked 'To what tavern will you go, sir?'
'Are we in Göttingen' said I.
'Ya wohl!'
'Then drive to the Crown!'
It was nearly two o'clock in the morning. I was a little vexed — it was too late!
I had taken a post-chaise at Nordhausen — and the postillion cracked like a little devil through Duderstadt and Heilingenstadt, and after all I was too late to see Ned that night!
When I got up in the morning I hurried on my long iron-grey surtout, and sallied forth in pursuit of Ned. I found his chambers — *Jew Alley* — 462!!!
'Der Herr Preble ist nicht zu Hause' (Mr. P. is not at home) — said the chamber-maid at the head of the stairs.
'I'll go in and wait,' said I.
In the antichamber stood a sofa with crimson plush covering: opposite hung a portrait of Napoleon, and in a corner a four-

---

[1] Among the earliest Americans who studied in Göttingen may be mentioned: Ticknor and Edward Everett (1815–1816); Bancroft (1818–1820); Motley (1832).

[2] From the first number of the 'Old Dominion Zeitung.'

stringed guitar. I entered Ned's room — his sitting room — study room. Splendidly lodged — thought I. In one corner stood a writing table and book-case, in another the stove, in another a sofa, with a round table before it — and in the fourth a clock ticked from a mahogany bureau. A checkered morning gown hung against the wall — here was a map of Germany, and there sundry long-stemmed porcelain pipes with a tobacco-pouch made of bladder. 'Taken to smoking' said I to myself — 'ganz eitel, sprach der Prediger.'

I shall not attempt to describe my feelings when at length Ned came in. I had taken him completely by surprise. And so here we are — two 'auld friends' talking about Portland — the glory and pride of our hearts — dear to us as the apple of our eye. What talk of old times! With three numbers of the *Yankee* before us — half an *Eastern Argus* — and an old *Eastport Sentinel*! Verily 'it is pleasant to sit down of an evening &c &c' vide Moorhead.

In my description of Ned's room I omitted most unaccountably the huge broad-swords — heavy yellow deer-skin gauntlets — and grey sword-proof shaking-Quaker hat, with tape strings. Ned — as represented in the cut — is arrayed in his olive-brown University cloak: fur cap without a rim — boots and spurs — reeking from the riding school. For my part, I am dressed in a claret-coloured double-breasted surtout. The cap on my head is Ned's — odious green — the same as if you should put a large green pocket-book on your head: Spanish Montero.

'Meeting here with an old and good friend has given a new elasticity to my spirits,' he wrote. They shared an enjoyment of the humors of German university life. In Craigie House is a quarto 'Journal,' kept by the two of them, filled with drawings, making fun of various persons and happenings. The chief outlet of their gaiety was the 'Old Dominion Zeitung,'[1] a manuscript journal which they dispatched to Portland at the end of each week — a mirror of doings in

---

[1] The term 'Old Dominion' is puzzling — especially as Longfellow uses it frequently at this time (also in *Outre-Mer*) in connection with his Virginia friends, the George Cookes, whom he met at Ariccia in 1828.

SKETCH OF THE TOWN HALL, GÖTTINGEN, BY LONGFELLOW, 1829

THE MEETING OF LONGFELLOW AND PREBLE IN GÖTTINGEN,
FEBRUARY 22, 1829

the town, liberally illustrated with pen-sketches by each of the pair. They are pictured as smoking and cruising about, or attending lectures; there is an account, by Longfellow, of a pompous student funeral, with an elaborate full-page drawing by his pen. A number of popular German student songs are transcribed. The chief function of the sheet was as an outlet to the wrath of the two young men because of the 'unfair treatment' shown to Longfellow by the Trustees of Bowdoin College. Longfellow had been informally assured of the professorship, with an understood salary of one thousand dollars, and was spending more than three full years, without expense to the institution, in fitting himself for his duties. Just as he was leaving Rome, he received a paralyzing letter from his father, informing him that the Trustees had decided that he was too young to be given a professorship, but that he would be made a tutor, with a salary of six hundred dollars. With this offer the young man vehemently refused to make terms, and the 'Old Dominion' is a very volcano of resentment — to which both friends heartily contributed.

Portly President Allen appears as a stout preserve-jar. Bowdoin is represented as an ass being whipped into the water by 'Public Opinion,' or carrying a load of 'northern darkness,' while treading on 'human understanding,' 'rights of man,' and the 'law of Bowdoin College'; again, the ass is shown kicking over a bucket labeled 'Professorship of Modern Languages.' Another picture is supplied with the following text, in Longfellow's hand:

> We have been creditably informed that a professorship being offered to a young man by the government of Bowdoin College on condition of his passing two years in Europe *at his own expence* — at the expiration of which time the situation of Tutor was offered him at little more than half a professor's salary! *We*

are happy to add that such a proposition has been treated with all the contempt it deserved!

Doubtless the finances of the college explain this action, though Longfellow's father, who was an influential Trustee, wrote at this time: 'On the subject of your connexion with Bowdoin College, I confess my feelings are very similar to yours.' He advised his son, however, to accept the terms for one year, during which he should demonstrate his worth to the institution. The young man faced firmly the probability that the appointment would fall through, though he still wished it, on honorable terms: 'no state of probation, no calling me a boy, and retrenching my salary.'

Longfellow's reactions to Göttingen were altogether agreeable: soon after arrival, he asks his father for permission to spend at least the summer there. Later, he writes that he likes Göttingen 'more and more daily.' There were almost no other Americans in the place, and there was very little contact with German students. Preble had made some associations before his friend's arrival, 'all from the studious class' — which always exists, rather quietly, in German universities. In his diary, which he kept in French, Longfellow wrote: 'There are almost no incidents in the life of a student'; 'I've kept close to my studies, almost to not going out of the house, and not allowing my eyes to wander from my book to look at the beautiful and modest Miss Young, my compatriot who lives across the street. There's a German song which fits me very well:

> Mir ist auf der Welt nichts lieber
> Als mein Stübchen, wo ich bin,
> Denn es wohnt mir gegenüber
> Eine schöne Nachbarin.'

'I have no other society than my books.' In *Hyperion*, touching on life in Heidelberg, he reverts to these days:

I suppose we shall lead about as solitary and studious a life here as we did of yore in little Göttingen, with nothing to amuse us, save our own daydreams.

The academic offerings during this semester were not favorable — there being no lectures on modern literary history. Two of his courses were given by Hofrat Heeren: *Alte Geschichte und Geschichte des neuern Europa samt seinen Colonien vom Anfang des XVI. Jahrhunderts an.* He also attended the lectures on *Naturrecht* by Professor J. A. Wendt, whom Brandl describes as 'der ästhetisch und juristisch angehauchte Philosoph.' Just how much the two friends were able to assimilate of these discourses may be open to doubt, but they doubtless learned some German during the process. In 1820, Heine had deplored the fact that Hofrat Benecke was the only professor in Göttingen who lectured on 'Old German Literature,' and that he had only nine hearers (one of whom was Heine), out of thirteen hundred students. Apart from the three hours daily spent at lectures, Longfellow devoted 'the remainder of his time' to the study of German under the guidance of this great Germanist (at whose home he also dined), and we may assume that it was very profitably spent. There is mention of a walking-tour to the ruin Plesse with Dr. Bode, who at one time had taught in Bancroft's school at Round Hill. He also made the personal acquaintance of Heeren and Blumenbach. He had not dropped his Romance studies: the library records show that nearly all the books he drew during his stay had to do with Spanish and Italian poetry; none of them concerned German letters. While at the University, he also began the writing of a 'Sketch-Book' of European experiences, giving expression to his earliest passion for Irving — a project completed four years later under the title, *Outre-Mer.*

There are many signs that he had already transcended the standards of American college life: he began to look down upon the illiberality and narrow views of academic leaders. An unpublished letter to his father indicates how the ferment of European educational ideals has begun to work:

GÖTTINGEN, *March* 10, 1829

My dear father, I have of late been reading a little and thinking much on the subject of Education. The public mind on both sides of the Atlantic seems at the present day to be directing its attention particularly to this point: I may say too its energies. The prevalent opinion is that in England and America the subject calls loudly for reform, but more so in America than elsewhere. And ours is an age and a country, in which the clearsighted and practical views of the community see nothing venerable even in antiquity itself, when errors and abuses take shelter beneath its gray hairs. — There is something so operative and thorough-going in freedom of thought and of the press — I may add, too, in the matter-of-fact way of thinking prevalent in our country — that to my mind the conclusion seems irresistible, that public opinion, which is directing its currents from all quarters of the land towards the abuses of education, as it exists with us,... will ere long undermine the foundations of our present erroneous systems, and sweep them from the face of the earth.

Germany and France may well boast of their schools and Universities. Good Heavens! what advantages have they not in these countries! Here indeed the gates of [opportunity] may be emphatically said to be swung wide open. There is a voice of free grace crying to all, that the fountains of their salvation are open. — May it soon be heard in our own happy land, swelling above the voice of worldly gain, and the roar of political strife.

What has heretofore been the idea of an University with us? The answer is a simple one: — Two or three large brick buildings — with a chapel, and a President to pray in it! — I say University, because with us University and College, have till now been almost synonymous terms. Mr. Jefferson it is true made a bold attempt — but it failed — if not totally at least in part — it failed — and why? — Because, with all due respect, he does

[20]

not seem to have begun right. He begun where every body else in *our* country would have begun, — by building college halls, and then trying to stock them with Students. — But that is not the way to found an University. European Universities were never founded in this manner. Indeed, as far as regards University buildings — one might live in Göttingen from one year's end to the other without having the slightest idea of its being the seat of a University. — No — it was by collecting together professors in whom the spirit moved — who were well enough known to attract students to themselves, and after they had assembled them capable of teaching them something they did not know before. It was so with the Italian, Spanish, German and French Universities — and when there is an American University, it must and will be so with that. Then, instead of seeing a new College ushered into existence every winter by a petition to the Legislature for funds to put up a parcel of Woolen-Factory buildings for students — we should see capital better employed in enriching the libraries of the country and making them *public!* — and instead of seeing the youth of our country chained together like galley slaves and 'scourged to their dungeon' — as it were — our eyes would be cheered by the grateful spectacle of mind throwing its fetters off — and education free from its chains and shackles.

Next to our own free government — I think the University of Paris the sublimest of all human institutions! — When I say the University of Paris I mean to include in the expression the Public Libraries, because tho' not in reality connected with the University, as they are open every day, one may derive the same advantages from them, as if they were. At the Garden of Plants are lectures on Botany, Nat. Hist., Mineralogy, &c. with illustrations from museums, and a garden containing almost every, if not every plant and animal in the world. At the Sorbonne are daily lectures on Geog., Statics, History, ancient and modern literature — the dead and living languages, Philosophy, &c. &c. &c. making the course more complete than even at Göttingen. — At the Law School are law lectures — and at the Medical college lectures in Surgery and medicine — with the privilege of accompanying the instructor through the Hospital under his care — assisting at his dissections — and even of having bodies for private dissection. This is a hasty and imperfect sketch of some of the advantages for a literary and scientific education at Paris: and all these advantages are perfectly and entirely *gratis*....

Take this and the German universities for models. Let two or three Professors begin the work — let them deliver lectures in some town (Portland seems to me better adapted for it than any other place in our part of the country) not in a village, not in the woods, if their lectures be worth anything, they will have hearers and disciples enough — and a *nucleus* will thus be formed, around which is to grow an University. — In the outset, lectures could not be *gratis* — no, the profits arising therefrom should be the Professor's support. Every one should rely upon his own talents for support, and his pay would in consequence be in proportion to his ability.

I am now coming to the application of my remarks. I told you in my last, that I wished to have nothing to do with Bowdoin. The system is too limited and superficial. Instead of going there I wish if possible to sow the seeds of an University after the model of those quoted above, in our own State and our own town. Portland is just the spot for an University (not a College) — it is neither too large nor too small. Yes, let Portland set an example to the whole U. States. Let us begin forth-with: As soon as I return — if the matter seems at all plausible — I mean to proffer my humble endeavours to the execution of such a plan — and put my shoulder to the wheel. The present is just the moment: we must take the tide there is in the affairs of men.

During the Easter vacation he took a full month from his German studies for a tour to Belgium, England, and France, and on June 6 he left Göttingen for home. In a letter to his friend Greene, he wrote: 'I was obliged to leave Göttingen on account of letters from home requiring my return' — but the 'requirement' was due rather to homesickness than to compulsion. His father had at once consented to his son's remaining through the summer at Göttingen, even advising him to study in Germany as long as possible, but urging his return by the end of September, 'before a voyage would become dangerous or uncomfortable' — and this counsel was invariably repeated.

In casting up the results of Longfellow's first German experiences, it is fair to say that the effects were decidedly relative, by no means revolutionary. 'The Rhine,' he wrote, 'is a noble river, but not so fine as the Hudson.' He had spent one month in Dresden, less than two and one-half in Göttingen, and these were broken into by a full month's sight-seeing in other lands.

A large Göttingen notebook (dated March 15, 1829, but showing also some entries from the Bowdoin period) is chiefly concerned with Spanish, French, Italian and Old English subjects. It contains one page of translation from Luther; one page copied from Heine's *Reisebilder* (I, 184: Ihr Auge... hervorlauschten), and one line from Voss's *Luise*.

His *Sprachgefühl* still lacks much of being a sure guide: the few extracts of German poetry which he wrote down are of painstaking, but by no means of impeccable, accuracy.

There are slips and solecisms enough in his records: Baron Löwenstein appears as 'Livingstern' and 'Livingstein'; Böttiger as 'Böticher'; he refers to 'the celebrated Naturalist, Blumingbach.' On leaving Göttingen, he practically omits all mention of German matters: the subsequent diary of his stay in England is written in Spanish.

He sailed homeward from Liverpool on July 1, 1829. A 'Certificate of Arrival' made out in England described him as: '23 years old; height, 5 ft., 8 in.; "chesnut" hair; fresh complexion; blue eyes; long nose; "chesnut" eyebrows.'

CHAPTER III

The Bowdoin Professorship

WHEN Longfellow had flatly refused a 'tutorship,' the Trustees of Bowdoin College compromised by electing the young man Professor — at eight hundred dollars, with the added duties of Librarian, at one hundred dollars a year. The latter office required his attendance in the library for only one hour each day; his teaching called for three recitations daily. In his first year he writes of 'correcting upward of forty French exercises daily,' and deplores the fact that his facility in speaking languages is slipping under him.

Up to the time of the poet's incumbency, a small amount of French was the only offering in modern languages. After his coming, French was required of all students through the Sophomore year. The Juniors might add an elective in Spanish or Italian. Not until 1831 was German added, as an elective for Juniors. In 1834, the Juniors were required to take two terms of Spanish or Greek, and the Seniors might elect, during their last two terms, Italian, German, or Hebrew.

In his second and third years at Bowdoin, Longfellow taught French, Spanish, Italian, and German — though it is uncertain how many students chose the last language. Manifestly, the subject did not occupy a very large place among his activities, though there is evidence that he maintained an interest in it. In his Inaugural Address as professor (September 2, 1830), he made the generalization: 'German poetry is characterized by its ideality, and a kind of vague and fanciful philosophy.' With no external stimulus, he continued to cultivate the German field.

[24]

On September 14, 1831, he married Mary Storer Potter, a lovely, well-bred girl, daughter of Judge Potter, of Portland. Among the books brought by her into the modest establishment was a copy of *The Literary Gem* (1827), which included translations from Goethe, Richter, and Körner.[1] In Longfellow's notebook of 1833 there are transcribed two stanzas from the *Ambraser Liederbuch*, and one from Sigmund von Birken (taken from Müller's *Bibliothek*). It likewise contains this translation of the first stanza of Johann Heermann's hymn, *Herzliebster Jesu*:

> What laws, my blessed Saviour, hast Thou broken
> That so severe a sentence should be spoken?
> How hast Thou 'gainst Thy Father's will contended?
> In what offended?

There were a few German books in the college library, and the professor of modern languages accumulated a respectable store: Eichhorn's *Culturgeschichte* and *Literaturgeschichte* (obtained through an acquaintance in Göttingen in 1830); the complete works of Klopstock, Gellert, Gleim, Goethe, Herder, Körner; good editions of the *Nibelungenlied* and *Heldenbuch*, and a number of comprehensive collections in the fields of literature, history, and language. From his Bowdoin notebook we glean two laudable, though halting, attempts at original German verse — the first dealing with his contentment in a secluded life; the second in a luscious Anacreontic mood:

> Verlangst du, Erdgeborn! ein ruhig Leben?
> Dem Himmel sey's gedankt — ich hab' es hier!
> Ich bin nicht reich — das Glück besteht nicht immer
> Im Reichtum — ach! sehr oft ist er die Quelle
> Von Kummer und von Sorgen — nein — Zufriedenheit
> Geht über Reichtum — und ich bin zufrieden —

[1] Higginson, 64.

Mein Herz kann keinen Kummer fassen — und
Verlang' ich nur dass man mich ruhig lasse! [1]

DIE SCHÖNHEIT

Stille! sie schlaft! — oh, eine Gottheit ist es!
Sehest du wie sanft das langes goldenes Haar,
Auf einem alabasternen Busen schwebt?
Sehest du die runden Formen — und die Farbe
Die susse Lilien und Rosen gleicht?
Den niedlich kleinen Fuss? — wie man die Mädschen
In Mahomet's Paradies' beschreibt?

It is evident that the young Professor of Modern Languages
had still to seek perfection in the mastery of the German
tongue.

His journal of December 2, 1834, records that he read one
of Wieland's *Psalms*. A translation of Körner's *Good Night*,
in *The Token* (1835), signed 'L,' shows every evidence of
being by Longfellow.

As a teacher, the young man showed much energy, and
introduced notable pedagogic improvements: he edited some
very sensible short textbooks for his classes in French, Spanish, and Italian, all of which showed the saving principle of
adapting elementary instruction to the live interest of young
students; these manuals qualify him for a place among the
authentic reformers of modern-language teaching. Of his
French grammar he writes to his father: 'nor is its being
adapted to the capacities of Children an objection: for let

---

[1] A yearning for undisturbed repose is characteristic. At this time he wrote:
'How sweet it will be, after being long jostled about the world, to enjoy once more
a calm and quiet life, and

> Nunc veterum libris, nunc somno et inertibus horis
> Ducere sollicitae jucunda oblivia vitae.'

Somewhat later:

'O for a lodge in some vast easy-chair, placed by a window!'

a man be as old and as learned in other things as you please, yet when he begins a language of which he knows nothing, he is a child.' These textbooks received high praise from Professor Ticknor.

During the Bowdoin period he published six major articles on European literature in the *North American Review*, and was in demand as a contributor to journals and 'special' volumes. The *Knickerbocker Magazine*, in New York, had passed, in May, 1834, into the hands of Longfellow's enthusiastic admirer, Lewis Gaylord Clark, who brought it into the front rank of American literary publications of its day. To this Longfellow sent three anonymous instalments, during 1834, of 'The Blank Book of a Country Schoolmaster,' in all, a set of eighteen detached observations on life, with which Clark was much pleased.

In spite of congenial duties, and the altogether happy marriage to a sweet, highly bred, intelligent girl, the isolation of Brunswick was becoming irksome to one who had drunk so long and so deep at the fountain-heads of Old-World civilization. As early as 1832, he is coquetting with the idea of becoming secretary to some European legation. Friend George Greene called his attention, at this time, to a professorship of Spanish in the New York University, and Longfellow, for two years, took steps to secure this. In July, 1833, he writes to Alexander Everett, making application for the post of Secretary of Legation at Madrid, and requesting Everett to communicate at once with the Secretary of State. In June, 1834, Mr. Justice Story, of the United States Supreme Court, and George Ticknor sent most laudatory recommendations for the New York position. In the same year, Longfellow made a trip to Northampton, with a view to taking over Bancroft and Cogswell's Round Hill School. In August, he writes many letters in pursuit of the professor-

ship of modern languages at the University of Virginia —
in all of these efforts he was disappointed.

The most significant document of Longfellow's restlessness
under 'small-town' surroundings is his 'Wondrous Tale of
a Little Man in Gosling Green,' which obtained, under an
assumed name, a prize of fifty dollars offered by Horace
Greeley, and was printed in Greeley's *New-Yorker* of November
1, 1834.[1] The narrow religionism, the petty gossip, the
isolation of 'Bungonuck' leave no doubt as to the feeling of
the poet concerning the limitations of Rural Maine. It
excites no wonder that the young professor kept this satire
a secret: it would have produced a prodigious fluttering in
the Brunswick dovecote. His father, most influential in
Bowdoin affairs, had moreover repeatedly expressed his fear
that the young professor was robbing his office by spending
time on merely literary work. In offering a book of sketches
for publication, Longfellow said: 'I do not wish to appear as
the author of the work.' *Outre-Mer* came out anonymously.

The first number of *Outre-Mer* appeared in July, 1833.
Longfellow had been planning the book for years, and it was
confessedly inspired by Irving's *Sketch-Book*. Of this American
classic the poet said in later life that he had been captivated
by it as a school-boy, 'spell-bound by its pleasant
humor, its melancholy tenderness, its atmosphere of revery.'
Small fascicles containing sketches of Spanish scenes (1827),
now preserved in Craigie House, show an early working of
this influence. When Longfellow settled in Göttingen (1829),
he informed his father: 'I am also writing a book — a kind
of Sketch-Book of France, Spain, and Italy'; — but he can
hardly have made much progress while in Germany. Alexander
Everett, editor of the *North American Review*, wrote

[1] This tale, with an account of its recent recovery, is printed in *American Literature* for April, 1931.

to Longfellow on April 27, 1832: 'Cannot you give us something in the form of travels or sketches in prose or verse about Spain? The subject is excellent, and almost new.' On March 9, 1833, Longfellow wrote to his friend Greene: 'I am writing a book, — a kind of Sketch-Book of France, Spain, Germany, and Italy;... If I conclude to publish it, I think I shall put it out in numbers or parts.'

Before the midale of July the first anonymous number had appeared, very noble in form — comparable to Irving's practice ('the fair clear type, which seemed an outward symbol of its style'); marbled paper covers, large pages, and a full page before each chapter, with a pertinent quotation (this feature dropped away from the finished work). The stanzas from Béranger, originally printed before the chapter *Coq-à-l'Ane*, suggest the deadening immobility of Brunswick:

> Voir, c'est avoir. Allons courir!
> Vie errante
> Est chose enivrante;
> Voir, c'est avoir. Allons courir!
> Car tout voir, c'est tout conquérir.

> Ton œil ne peut se détacher,
> Philosophe,
> De mince étoffe,
> Ton œil ne peut se détacher,
> Du vieux coq de ton vieux clocher.

It was beautifully printed by J. Griffin, in Brunswick, his type-setter being one Theodore S. McClellan. Longfellow adds a note to the manuscript:

> Mr. Griffin! Mr. Griffin!
> If that *devil* Theodore
> Tears my copy any more,
> I will tear him in a *jiffin*,
> Mr. Griffin!

[29]

The thrift which was prescribed in the humble *ménage* is illustrated by the fact that the manuscript for the first half of the work is written entirely on the backs of variegated old letters (the latest being of date January 28, 1833). The 'Epistle Dedicatory' was written four times. An alternative title was: 'The Pilgrim from the Land of Steady Habits.' The ultimate place of the book in literature will not concern us here: in his own copy, Longfellow wrote pathetically: '*Laudatur et alget!*' Its archaisms are more conscious and affected than is the case in Irving's book. Longfellow confesses, in correspondence, that he is doing 'fine writing,' and finds it hard. Hawthorne derived much pleasure from it. A London reviewer spoke of its 'elegantly pensive stories.' As a book of travel, the work is assuredly not incisive, critical, and stabbing, as, for instance, Zangwill's *Italian Fantasies*. To his friend Pierce, who gave it publicity in Portland, the author wrote: 'Much obliged to you for the puff. Blow, breezes, blow!'

While *Outre-Mer* is concerned with Romance matters, there is some precipitate from German experiences: the author speaks of 'having trimmed his midnight lamp in a German university.' In describing a night-journey in a French diligence, he translates a stanza from *Lenore*, which quite misses the rugged slap-bang of Bürger's stalwart ballad.[1] A quotation from A. W. von Schlegel, referring to ancient German songs, the *Nibelungen*, and the *Hofbuch*, may have been derived from an English translation which was then in the Bowdoin Library. The 'German moralist' quoted in 'A Tailor's Drawer,' has been identified as Jean Paul Richter by Mr. Campbell — thus giving us the first definite sign of Longfellow's reactions to an author who was

[1] Longfellow's attention may have been called to Bürger by Irving's allusion in the *Sketch-Book* ('Spectre Bridegroom').

destined to hold a unique place in his esteem. The few words of the 'German Allegory' seem also akin to Jean Paul, and the thesis, 'music is the universal language of mankind — poetry their universal pastime and delight,' may have come from Herder. There is one direct quotation from Goethe's *Werther*, and two from the First Part of *Faust* — but such scattered instances cannot make a 'German work' of *Outre-Mer*. At the close, the author touches on Trieste, Vienna, Dresden, Leipsic and Göttingen — but these are merely diary jottings: the professor was too much occupied with his impending European trip to elaborate them.

CHAPTER IV

The Second Stay in Europe

THE unexpected tender of the Smith Professorship of Modern Languages in Harvard University, suggested by George Ticknor, and made in a letter from President Quincy of December 1, 1834, dropped into the unsatisfying Bowdoin scene like a voice from heaven. The letter closed with the words: 'Should it be your wish, previously to entering upon the duties of the office, to reside in Europe, at your own expense, a year or eighteen months for the purpose of a more perfect attainment of the German, Mr. Ticknor will retain his office till you return.'

Thrice welcome as this call was, the cautious young man replied: 'Before accepting, let me learn more of the duties of the office.' He conferred with his prudent father, as usual, and journeyed to Cambridge, to survey the land. There was, however, little hesitation: the Brunswick home was dismantled, goods were stored, and on April 10, 1835, the professor and his young wife sailed for England. The party included two young friends, Miss Clara Crowninshield [1] and Miss Mary C. Goddard. London was reached by the middle of May; the three weeks spent there were given to sightseeing, as well as to the enjoyment of many social attentions from significant people. [2] Very soon after reaching London, Longfellow (who had been introduced by Emerson) called on Mrs. Carlyle at Chelsea: [3]

---

[1] Miss Crowninshield's copious diaries (preserved by her granddaughter, Frau Clara von Jordan, of Herischdorf, Silesia) give many details of the entire stay in Europe.

[2] The travelers met, among others, John Bowring, the Lockharts, Babbages, Lady Morgan, Lady Seymour, Lady Dudley Stuart.

[3] MS. journal, May 21, 1835.

Speaking of Hayward, the prose-translator of Goethe's Faust, she said she did not like the book, and did not think the translator equal to his task.

'But in his Preface he animadverts harshly upon the defects of other translators.'

'Oh yes, indeed; detraction is the element in which he moves and breathes and has his being.'

On May 30, Carlyle called on the Longfellow party. Of this visit Mary Longfellow wrote: [1]

Mr. Carlyle, of Craigenputtock, was soon after announced, and passed a half-hour with us, much to our delight. He has very unpolished manners and a broad Scottish accent, but such fine language and beautiful thoughts that it is truly delightful to listen to him. He invited us to take tea with them at Chelsea, where they now reside. We were as much charmed with Mrs. C. as with her husband. She is a lovely woman, with very simple and pleasing manners. She is also very talented and accomplished; and how delightful it is to see such modesty combined with such power to please.

The same evening the party took tea at the Carlyles. Next day Longfellow wrote in his diary:

Passed the morning over a coal fire, reading Carlyle's Life of Schiller; a work of rare merit — written by one who entered *con amore* into his subject. It is altogether a fine biographical sketch; though the author speaks slightingly of it, and 'wonders how anyone can read so tame and colorless a production.' *June 1.*: It is nearly two o'clock in the morning, and I have just finished The Life of Schiller; a truly noble delineation of the life, character and writings of that great and good man. I shall lie down to sleep with my soul quickened, and my good resolutions strengthened.

A day or two later, Mrs. Carlyle took the ladies of the party to visit the studio of Chantrey, the sculptor, and on

[1] *Life*, I, 208.

the following morning Mr. Longfellow had breakfast in Chelsea: [1]

> Breakfasted at Mr. Carlyle's in a quiet, friendly way... He stepped out of the room for a few minutes and I asked his wife if he considered Goethe the greatest man that ever lived. She replied:
> 'O yes, I believe he does indeed. He thinks him the greatest man that ever lived, excepting only Jesus Christ.'
> Mrs. Carlyle is also a German scholar. She told me her husband was much pleased with what she said of her own impressions of Schiller and Goethe: — 'What I read of Schiller makes me shed tears; but what I read of Goethe, I read a second time.' — Her husband wrote this to Goethe, who expressed himself much gratified; as his aim was to make people think, and not to move their sympathies. Goethe she thinks the *greater* man; Schiller the most *loveable*.

The professor-elect was minded to give Harvard full measure in the matter of an equipment in the Germanic languages, and turned his course, first, to Scandinavian territory. The journey was by ship to Hamburg, where Shakespeare's *Kaufmann von Venedig*, in Schlegel's translation (Seidelmann as Shylock), was seen at the City Theater. The months of July and August were spent, rather drearily, though not without some friendly social attentions, in Stockholm, while Swedish was vigorously attacked under the direction of one of the Upsala professors. Longfellow's command of German was adequate as a medium of intercourse with Swedish friends — though the ladies of the party lacked this resource. On leaving Sweden by steamer, Longfellow was mildly amused by the fact that the Pastor of Lund beguiled the time on Sunday by playing cards with some of the King's officers; this evoked his comment: 'Hurra! lustig in die Welt hinein!' He wavered for a while between Berlin

[1] MS. journal, June 3, 1835.

and Bonn as a place for his German studies during the winter, but by September 20 had decided on Heidelberg. Only thirteen days were spent in Copenhagen, but during this time Longfellow managed to secure lessons in Icelandic from Professor Rafn, and in Danish from one of the royal librarians. He also bought Weber's work *On Teutonic Romances*. From Copenhagen Miss Goddard returned home, on account of the death of her father. While in the Danish capital, Mary was taken ill, but recovered sufficiently to proceed on the journey. There were two days spent in Kiel, where Longfellow called on Professor Falck, and discussed with him the North-German dialects. In Amsterdam travel was halted because of Mary's increasing sickness: she took to bed, medical aid was summoned, and a nurse engaged. During the three weeks in Amsterdam, her husband read Tegnér's *Frithiof's Saga*, in the original, took lessons in Dutch, and made his first acquaintance with the Low-German epic, *Reynke de Vos*, of which he wrote:

I have got to-night a book which keeps me late from my bed. How very beautifully the old poem commences:

'Twas in the time of Whitsontide
When field and forest far and wide,
Were all so green with leaves and grass,
And many a bird right merry was,
Singing in hedge and woodland bowers; –
The herbs were sprouting and the flowers
Sweet-smelling here and there,
And the weather clear and the day so fair!

Verily, these old German poets were like the birds themselves. They sing in sunshine among leaves and flowers!

An encouraging rally on the part of the sufferer led to hopes of an early recovery, the doctor decided to discontinue his visits, and the party took carriage to Rotterdam. Im-

[35]

mediately after arrival, a return of illness occurred. Once more there were alternations of hope and depression; on November 4 was recorded: 'Mary is recovering famously.'

On October 28, Longfellow called on the Reverend Doctor Joseph L. Bosworth, an English clergyman, at the time in charge of the English church in Rotterdam, one of the most meritorious earlier workers in the field of Anglo-Saxon philology. They discussed grammars, dictionaries, and dialects, and the visit led to a close association during the six weeks' stay. At Bosworth's request, Longfellow furnished him with a somewhat extensive chapter on the Swedish dialect of Dalecarlia, which was included in the Preface of Bosworth's monumental *Dictionary of the Anglo-Saxon Language* published in London in 1838. A footnote reads: 'Professor Longfellow, of Harvard University, Cambridge, America, who has recently returned from Sweden, was so obliging as to draw up this notice of the Dalecarlian dialect, October, 1835' — which gives some indication of the strenuousness of the studies pursued in Stockholm. German was not neglected:

> Looked over the Poems of Uhland. His little Ballad of 'Der schwarze Ritter' is beautiful. His imagination seems to be steeped in the poetry of the past — the songs of the Minnesingers.[1]

Within a month, Longfellow was conversing quite freely in Dutch.

Mary's serene death occurred, unexpectedly, on November 29. On the preceding day, Longfellow wrote: 'It is a great consolation to us to have Clara here. She takes the place of a sister... and does all she can to cheer and soothe us.' Dr. Bosworth was summoned during her last moments,

[1] MS. journal, Nov. 1, 1835.

and prayed at the bedside. Her body was embalmed, arrangements were made for its transport on a ship soon to sail for Boston, and the disconsolate young widower took his way, with Miss Crowninshield, up the Rhine to Heidelberg, which was reached on December 11. Passing through Bonn, he paid his respects to August Wilhelm von Schlegel:

> I was shown up into a small room, furnished with a desk or two — a table, sofa and chairs. On one of the desks was a bust of Schlegel. The servant maid threw a few faggots into the chimney, and kindled a fire. In a few minutes enter Schlegel: an old man, stooping under the burden of some three score years. He wore a little black scull-cap; a frilled shirt, without cravat; a loose, brown or rather clarat surtout, drab pantaloons and cloth slippers. His forehead broad and high — eyes large — and the expression of his countenance intellectual and pleasant. He rather lectured than conversed; so I shall not pretend to record what he said. He was, to tell the truth, rather discursive; and I could not get him upon any topic of interest to myself. Still I was much gratified to see the translator of Shakespeare. He is very much of a gentleman — and takes snuff from an ornamented box of tortoise shell.

He remained in Heidelberg half a year, at the pleasant home of Frau Himmelhahn, the second house west of the Karlstor. ('Frau Himmelhahn,' the aged Heidelberg gossip in *Hyperion*, was discreetly altered to 'old Frau Himmelauen' in later editions). Miss Crowninshield found shelter with the romantic-minded Hepp family, in a home which provided Longfellow's chief refuge during his stay. There were other boarders, cultivated and socially minded, and gatherings for whist and music were of almost daily occurrence; in this circle he bore the name, 'Wilhelm Meister.'

In the earlier months, he was well-nigh crushed under the burden of his loss. The weather, too, was cold and depressing. His 'escape' came by way of a devotion, with an incredible grim persistence, to the chief object of his stay, the mastery of the German language and literature 'from its origin.' In addition, he supervised Clara's German studies, in which she gained no mean mastery. Among other things, she made, with his assistance, a manuscript album of thirty-seven beautifully-written German songs, with full musical accompaniments (still preserved). Letters were presented to influential professors of the University, though Longfellow soon decided that 'its literary faculty is null and void.' There were return invitations to professorial homes. He waited on Bertrand, Mittermaier, Gervinus,[1] Reichlin-Meldegg, and Schlosser — 'who made me a long discourse upon German Literature at the present day: — the Romantic School, and the "Young Germany," whose chief apostle is Heine. Wolfgang Menzel got a slap, as smiting right and left in his criticism, and handling matters "*ganz burschikos*." ' The Librarian, Dr. Umbreit, laid before him some of the manuscript treasures of the University. A day or two after arriving, Longfellow called on William Cullen Bryant, who was living in Heidelberg with his family.

> He seemed well pleased to see a countryman. He was pleasant and talkative — though he has little animation. He has a good face — calm and thoughtful — with a mild, light-blue eye, that is very expressive.

Bryant was soon compelled to return to the United States, but Longfellow kept up the friendliest association with his wife and daughters. He did not keep entirely aloof from the somewhat grotesque doings of the Heidelberg students, viewing them with the mildly ironic detachment of the self-contained New-Englander.

On December 18 the diary records: 'Passed the morning

---

[1] This eminent authority left Heidelberg for Göttingen, early in 1836.

at home, looking over a little work containing Schleiermacher's Letters on Friedrich Schlegel's romance of *Lucinde*.' Before the end of 1835, Longfellow's command of German was sufficiently perfect to enable him to 'hold his own eloquently in German discussions' — as an American living in Heidelberg at the time testified.[1] Such an occasion was found at the home of the Hepps, where he argued at length with the oldest daughter, Julie, on the comparative merits of Goethe and Schiller.

Despite these many-sided occupations, the cloud of depression continued to hang over him: he brooded over the parental objections to this European trip, and, on the last day of the year 1835, 'saw his father's face looking towards him, sorrowfully and beseechingly.'

During February, 1836, he was chiefly busied with preparing a 'Handbook' or 'Syllabus' of the 'Literature of the Middle Ages,' from the close of the fifth to the close of the fifteenth centuries. In the process of getting it up, he 'nearly froze himself to death in the University Library.' This work, which was prepared for printing,[2] exists in a bound manuscript volume at Craigie House. It is a running chronological list, with comments and references to a long array of sources. There is one original critical amendment to an article in the *Revue Germanique*. Considering the amount of time the author had to put on this effort, it shows enormous industry. But the pages of his diary also reveal a zeal in reading that is phenomenal: a mere catalogue is sufficiently impressive.

He studied Wackernagel's *Altdeutsches Lesebuch* in five volumes ('it's the best book of the kind I have ever met

---

[1] This facility was never lost, and called forth the admiration of all German visitors to Craigie House.

[2] According to S. Longfellow (I, 227) it was printed in the (N.Y.) *Eclectic Review* in 1841. I have been unable to find it.

with'); Grimm's *Deutsche Grammatik* (3 vols.), the *Ludwigslied*, *Annolied*, parts of the *Nibelungenlied* ('this old Epic of the thirteenth century deserves an entire translation into English' — a task worthily carried out by Professor Needler in 1904); certain of the *Minnelieder*; Flögel's *Geschichte der komischen Literatur*; Rosenkranz's *Geschichte der Poesie*,[1] and Schubert's *History of the Soul*. Grimm's and Musaeus' *Märchen*, Görres' *Volksbücher*, *Des Knaben Wunderhorn*, Erlach's *Volkslieder*, and *Till Eulenspiegel* brought him into contact with the soul of the common people. He read from Herder 'under the garden trees'; likewise Lessing's *Nathan* (which he saw given in Mannheim), *Emilia Galotti* ('the catastrophe is foreseen from the first act; and the author proceeds to carry forward the single action of the piece without turning to the right or left'), and *Wie die Alten den Tod gebildet*. With Clara he reviewed *Faust*; reading also *Egmont*, *Werther*, *Wilhelm Meister*, *Dichtung und Wahrheit*, *Das Märchen* and *Die Geschwister* ('though trifling as a literary production, has one or two touches of pathos, that brought tears into my eyes, and recalled the affection and devoted love of one that is gone'). Goethe's lyrics, some fifteen of which were included in Clara's album, were not neglected: he tells of encountering

a stream which might have suggested to Goethe the poem of 'The Youth and the Mill-brook.' When I heard the stream gushing among stones and rocks and saw the mill-wheel turning in the current with its never-ceasing plash! plash! — the words of the beautiful song sounded in the voice of the waters. It was for the moment a water-nymph [2] that sung.... To understand and feel German poetry you must see a German landscape. Many sweet little poems of the Germans are words to which the song of birds — the rustling of leaves — and the gurgle of cool waters —

[1] A passage in the preface plays an important part in *Hyperion*, I, vii.

[2] Here there is perhaps an added touch from Wilhelm Müller's *Schöne Müllerin*.

are the appropriate music. It is the music of Nature, to which man has composed the words.[1]

Of Werther he wrote:

The language and imagery are beautiful. In England and America the book is sneered at. I think it is not understood. In one or two places the author has suffered his love for simple homely nature to carry him a little too far; as Wordsworth has done in his poetry. They have both been laughed at by persons who have intellect without tenderness of heart, and by those who have neither; but, not by the few who have both. Thus for example, when Goethe describes the delight his Werther felt in going out into his garden at sunrise to gather green-peas — in sitting down to shell them, while he read his Homer — in choosing his sauce-pan, buttering his peapods, and stirring them over the kitchen fire — it requires a mind of peculiar tone to enter into the *ideal* of such a scene, and with the hero 'powerfully feel, how the superb lovers of Penelope slew oxen and swine, hewed them piece-meal and roasted them.' To the great majority of readers the whole transaction is ridiculous in a romance; a very few only will see therein a forthshadowing of simple, patriarchal life....

After all, such books are not favorites with me. The impression they leave in the soul is one of unrest and pain. This is not the company I love to keep. I should shun the society of a person, who with all Werther's admirable qualities of heart and mind — talked and acted as he does. Therefore such books do not lie 'close to my heart and mine eye.'

The following passage (from the journal) is symptomatic of Longfellow's earlier stage of criticism:

Goethe certainly loves to describe the painfully interesting scenes of human frailty: — and they take a strong hold upon our sensibilities, because we also are human. There is a living reality and truth about his works, which none can deny. Human nature is seen there as in a mirror — but alas! only in its degradation; not in its brightness, and strength, and purity. His admirers

[1] Some of this material is used in *Hyperion*, II, VII.

say, this is a true picture of life; and when they have said this, they think that they have said all — that all objections are answered. But who has told them, that books are to be nothing more than an exact reflection of what passes in real life? There is enough misery in the world to make our hearts heavy: — in books let us have something more than this — something to strengthen and elevate and purify us. Schiller, the beautiful Schiller, does this. He is the prophet of the ideal — Goethe the prophet of the real. To these two great poets may be applied the image of Collins:

> *This* raised a mortal to the skies,
> *That* brought an angel down.

Schiller-reading (partly with and for Clara) included *Don Carlos, Wallenstein,* and *The Thirty Years' War.* He read a biography of Bürger, and some of his ballads: 'The "High Song of the Only One" is a masterpiece of harmony.' He was very sympathetic to the light melancholy of Hölty and Matthisson; with Clara he read Novalis' *Heinrich von Ofterdingen.* Hoffmann's Tales, Chamisso's *Peter Schlemihl,* Fouqué's *Undine,* Tieck's *Elves, Rotkäppchen, Runenberg,* and *Peter of Provence* offered typical examples of later Romanticism. Two stories by Carové (the 'one who dwelleth by the castled Rhine' in Longfellow's poem, *Flowers*) led to the comment:

The first called 'The Story Without an End' — an exquisite little prose-poem, in which are described the feelings which we may imagine to fill the heart of a little child, who goes out among flowers and singing birds, and full of childish delight in its own thoughts holds converse with all the beautiful living things around it. The other tale is in a different style — part humorous, part pathetic — and is rather a sketch than a Tale. It is entitled 'A Day in the Belfry of Andernach.' It is very spirited and interesting. Carové lives in Frankfort. He is a mystic; — and has a dreamy, visionary mind. A devout Catholic.

[42]

To these must be added Heine's *Romantic School*, poems of Klopstock, the Stolbergs, Hebel, M. Frey, Zedlitz and Salis-Seewis, and, particularly, the works of Jean Paul (*Campaner-Tal*, *Flegeljahre*, *Titan*). Much could be added from the diary to the characterization of Jean Paul in *Hyperion*:

> This eagle of German literature is not content to sweep through the bright fields of pure air and bright sunshine — but he must dart into the thunder-clouds, and hide himself in mists and vapors. He soars beyond our ken — and we only hear his scream.

Incidentally, he began an article on modern German drama for the *North American Review* — which never came to publication.

Such zeal could only lead to exhaustion — and on May 14 comes the pardonable entry: 'I am growing tired of being cooped up here in Heidelberg — beautiful as it is. I feel a strong desire to be once more on the wing.' A few days later, the (here much condensed) outburst:

> Verily the inhabitants of Heidelberg are not a very cleanly and sweet-scented race! Every front entry smells worse than a stable.... The Hauptstrasse is but a mile long; — there are all kinds of utter abominations on the sidewalks.... The English are by far the most cleanly and decent people on the face of the earth; — including ourselves under the name of English.

It was getting time for moving on from Heidelberg! Obviously, Longfellow had not become completely Teutonized — as certain Germans do falsely boast.

Before he left for the south, he translated Aloys Schreiber's song, *An die Glocke*.

On June 20 comes the entry: 'Torpor steals over me again, and the monotonous every-day life begins anew. My mind has lost its sensibility and does not feel the spur. I cannot

study: and therefore think I had better go home. Perhaps
the air of the Fatherland will do me good.' — What wonder!
He left Heidelberg on June 25 for a month's solitary trip
in Germany, Austria, and Switzerland. The experiences of
this excursion are set down so circumstantially in *Hyperion*,
that that work may serve as the Baedeker of the trip. At
the first station on the journey south, he records in tolerable
German:

> Wie bin ich so froh, dass ich wieder auf der Reise bin. Das
> Rollen des Wagens hat mich schon in eine gute Stimmung
> gebracht. Der Postillion fährt aber gar langsam. Wir kommen
> nicht von der Stelle. Das Wetter auch ist nicht günstig. Es hat
> die ganze Nacht geregnet; und jetzt in der Morgendämmerung
> ziehen grosse Wolken wie Riesengespenster durch das enge
> Thal hindurch.
> Dort oben auf dem Berge steht Dilsburg, und unten der
> grüne Neckar schlängelt sich 'ganz sachte fort durch Wiesen.'
> Der trübe Himmel wird almälig heller. Der Postillion legt
> seinen Mantel ab, und Lerchen schwingen sich schwirrend in
> die Höhe.

In Stuttgart he called on the sculptor, Dannecker, and
went in pursuit of Uhland, but, after inquiring through the
whole street to which he was directed, gave up in despair.
Munich was the next objective, and from there the journey
to Salzburg was undertaken in a coach: 'We were four in-
side.... Gilparzer [*sic*], a poet from Vienna, an insignificant
man in appearance; but a very pleasant one in reality.'
The other chief stages were St. Gilgen, Innsbruck, Con-
stance, Zurich, Brunnen, the Furca and Grimsel passes,
Interlaken and Thun. Here, on July 20, he fell in with Mr.
Nathan Appleton, of Boston, who was traveling with his
daughters Mary and Frances, and an invalid nephew. He
conversed with Mr. Appleton, but the Boston family was
journeying in another direction — so he continued, with a

prophetic reluctance, his lonely way, recording: 'Every hour my heart aches.'

After a solitary tour of ten days through the regions of Lake Geneva and Chamonix, he made his way back to Interlaken, where the Appletons were established in an attractive *pension*; on the day after arrival, he 'moved in' under the same roof.

Miss Frances Appleton was, perhaps, Boston's most desirable *partie*: young, lovely, cultured, charming in mind and conversation, rich; from her own diary we have evidence that she was not, at first, particularly edified by the intimate addition to the family group of the older professorial widower, already known as a writer, whose young wife had died only eight months before. However, Providence shaped affairs according to its own plans. A comparison of two diaries shows that natural selection followed its inexorable laws:

On the second day, Longfellow wrote: 'Walked with Miss Fanny. She sketched. After tea talked incessantly with M. A. She entered with spirit into the conversation. It was delightful.... I now for the first time enjoy Switzerland.' Fanny records: 'Have a nice walk with Mr. Longfellow to the old bridge.... Sketched.... A nice talk, delicious twilight.'

On August 3, the augmented group began a carriage-tour, to Lake Lucerne, Zurich, and Schaffhausen — where a long stay ensued, because of the rapidly failing health, and (before long) the death of the invalid cousin. Some notes of this journey are revelatory: Longfellow wrote, 'My propitious star placed me in Mr. Appleton's travelling carriage with the two young ladies, who are all intellect and feeling.... I hardly looked from the carriage window. The time glided too swiftly away; for our conversation was of all that is gentle and fair; and we read the *Genevieve* of Coleridge, and the *Christabel*: and many other scraps of song; and little ballads of Uhland, simple and strange. And all this to me is a passion; — a delight, strong and unchanging.' Fanny's account: 'Read German, Coleridge, etc., all the morning and so saw no scenery.'

Later in the same day Longfellow wrote, 'My soul was filled with peace and gladness' — but not many hours afterwards comes the enigmatic entry: '... and finally — Damnation!' It needs no very constructive imagination to infer that the young widower had permitted himself some expression of sentimentality — and had been effectively checked; as may also be easily deduced from chapter nine of the third book of *Hyperion*.

At Zurich Longfellow wrote: 'I translated Uhland's ballad of the *Castle by the Sea*, with the assistance of Lady Fanny, who was scribe on the occasion, and made some of the best lines.' Before reaching Schaffhausen, 'we got out of our carriage and walked a mile or two. The scene was perfectly quiet; a breathless stillness as if all Nature were at prayer; and, as Fanny said, the trees looked as if they were standing up in their pews to sing' — a passage showing the embellishment due to heightened emotion, for Miss Fanny herself wrote: 'A silence as if the trees were asleep in their pews.'

While faithfully occupied with cheering the failing invalid in Schaffhausen, Longfellow found time to read *Modern Characteristics*, a work on contemporary German men-of-letters: 'The sketch of Hoffmann of Fallersleben is capital.' More than a fortnight of unmixed happiness had been experienced, when there came to Schaffhausen a rather peremptory letter from Clara Crowninshield, marooned at Heidelberg with the Bryant family, and 'out of patience waiting for an escort to America.' Conscience-stricken at

FRANCES ELIZABETH APPLETON
By G. P. A. Healy

his oblivion to the faithful Clara, Longfellow absented himself instantly from felicity, and posted straight for the German university city, which he reached in three days. Shortly thereafter, he accompanied the Bryant family and Miss Crowninshield to Paris, and sailed with her from Havre on October 10. While in Paris, he alludes to a passage in *Werther*; also there is an unexpected transcription of a well-known German *Volkslied*, sole entry in the journal for September 28:

> Kömmt a Vogel geflogen,
> Setzt sich nieder auf ma Fuss;
> Hat a Zettel in dem Goschel
> Und von Liebsten a Gruss.
>
> Lieber Vogel, flieg' weiter,
> Nimm a Brief mit und a Kuss,
> Und ig kann die nit begleiten,
> Weil ig hier bleiben muss.

— Had Fanny imparted some communication?

CHAPTER V

Life as Professor in Harvard

EARLY in December, 1836, Longfellow took lodgings in Cambridge — eager for action, encumbered with a debt of one thousand dollars, and girding himself for his impending duties as 'Smith Professor of the French and Spanish Languages and Literature, and Professor of Belles Lettres,' duties which were to begin with the second college term, in the second week of January, 1837.

The academic year consisted of three terms: Commencement came on the last Wednesday in August, following a six-weeks' vacation. The first term extended from the Friday after Commencement to the Wednesday preceding Christmas — some sixteen weeks. The second term, of thirteen weeks, began in the early part of January; the third ('summer') term began about the middle of April, and lasted thirteen weeks — or until the middle of July. No modern languages were accepted for entrance credit; they were required throughout the Sophomore and Junior years; of Seniors, during their first and second terms. These languages (French, Spanish, Italian, Portuguese, German) were taught by foreign-born instructors. The duty of the Professor was to supervise the native teachers, and to give 'lectures during the course of the year,... which specified classes are required to attend.' Longfellow was announced to deliver such lectures 'on the French, Spanish and German Languages and Literature.' He wrote his father, 'I think I shall have nothing to do but lecture'; after beginning the work, he reported: [1] 'I have no classes to hear in College

[1] February 1, 1837.

[48]

and in all probability shall never be required to hear any.' The new head of the modern-language department was assuredly not one of those traditional professors 'who see the world but on a Sunday.' In sharp contrast with those traditions, he was a pronounced dandy in attire: 'The reason of my drawing so much in Paris was that I got an abundant supply of clothing there.'[1] Just before beginning his work, he wrote to 'Tom' Appleton (Fanny's popular brother) in Paris, to buy him 'one dozen light-colored kid gloves at Privat's on the Rue de la Paix, near the Boulevard.' From his sister he asks a 'frilled shirt' and 'dickeys.' 'The first thing that meets your admiring gaze [in his lodgings] is the author of Outre Mer reclining on a sofa, in a striped calamanco morning gown; slippers red.' Following his visit to London, in 1842, Dickens wrote him: 'The hosier, the trowsers-maker, and the coat-cutter have all been at the point of death;... it was exhaustion, occasioned by early rising — to wait upon you!'

He was a social favorite, both in the 'village' and across the Charles. His journal speaks of his 'inveterate habit of town-going,' and 'an incontinent lot of walking into town.' At the end of his second year he wrote: 'For nearly two years I have not studied at night — save now and then at intervals. In Winter go much into Boston society. Into Cambridge society almost never.' Charles Follen, a cultured German exile, the first professor of German at Harvard, had testified admiringly, a few years before:[2] 'Boston's aristocracy is chiefly of talent, wealth, moral habits, good manners and courtesy.' We may believe that there was a still stronger magnet which drew the Cambridge professor to Beacon Hill. An unaddressed letter, written at the end of his first year,

[1] December 7, 1836.
[2] *Life of C. Follen*, I, 237.

points clearly to Mary Appleton [1] as its recipient, and indicates that she was his trusty friend-at-court:

Mein liebes Fräulein.
I return Heine [2] with thanks manifold, and a request, that at some future day, you will lend me all the volumes; as I want to read them again, and am tempted to write a review of the whole.[3]
Verily he is a beautiful writer, and one of the greatest *painters in words.* Dont you think so? The origin of German Popular Tales in Vol. 1, and the description of the Italian itinerant musicians in Vol. 3 are exquisite. He is a Lord Byron in Prose; with all the fire, wit, feeling of the English poet, and more pathos.
As to the *Faustian* episode of 'Belfagor in Beacon Street,' [4] I fear to undertake it now. I am too serious and sad. The devil would enter, as he does in the old Miracle Plays, shouting 'Ho! ho! ho!' and that is not the vein for your gentlemanly Belfager; who as I had conceived the part, was to be nowise Satanic, but rather a soft and Pelham-devil, with french boots and *gants de beurre frais.*
Meanwhile I am delighted to hear, that you intend to note down your passing thoughts on the Faust of Old Humbug, as some of the gentle critic craft are pleased to call the brave old German. I wish you would write them in my book instead of your own. At all events, let me read them, wont you? I have just finished the Second part; and have no more Lectures till January, when I begin Dante [5] — that is the Purgatorio and Paradiso, to please my imagination with sweeter visions than the Inferno; which with all its horrors I make over to Dr. Bachi [6] forever. I am tired of *Infernos.* I shall however write out, and very soon, (I intended to do it last week) a Lecture upon the

[1] Fanny's older sister. She married Mr. Robert J. Mackintosh, son of Sir James Mackintosh.

[2] On January 17, 1840, Mary Appleton Mackintosh speaks of German books (*Wilhelm Meister*, Musaeus) which L. had lent her.

[3] Such a study of Heine was published by L. in *Graham's Magazine*, March, 1842.

[4] In La Fontaine's *Belphegor*, the hero sues a proud beauty for ten years; at the end of this time, she grants the reply, '*Oui.*'

[5] He gave his introductory lecture on Dante on January 15, 1838.

[6] Instructor in Italian.

Faust. I think one will be enough: and this you shall certainly see, if you think it wont tire you to death. There is only one impediment in the way. I was imprudent enough to take up Dante the other day; and he excites me more than any other poet. I hate to turn back to Goethe. But the lecture must be written; and I think I had better settle with the *Adversary*, while I am in the way with him. Tell me, how can I stop midway in an Introductory Lecture on Christian Dante to take up Heathen Goethe? — So much for not being systematic. Truly I have a pretty medley in my brain this week; namely Dante, Goethe, Henry Heine, Paul de Kock, Scott's Life, and the Death Song of Regnar Leather-Breeches,[1] the Iceland Scald. These have been mixed up from day to day during the week in a style which 'Shenstone might have envied.' There were also some other ingredients which I have forgotten; equal to 'Pickwick and the Pequot Wars.'

And what have you been doing in the bright parlor? Shall I sit there no more with you, and read in pleasant books! Are those bright autumnal mornings gone forever?

Ach, du schöne Seele! Es wird mir gar traurig zu Muthe, wenn ich daran denke, und sehe, wie der schöne Traum dahin zieht, — wie die Wolke sich theilt, und in Thränen zerfliesst, und um mich wird alles so leer, und in meiner Seele eine dunkle Nacht — eine dunkle sternlose Nacht! — Und dass hab' ich Dir auf Deutsch sagen müssen, weil eine fremde Sprache ist eine Art von Dämmerung und Mondlicht, worin man den Frauenzimmern allerlei sagen kann — und so herzlich treu! Eben so herzlich grüsse mir die liebe, liebe Fanny, die ich immer liebe, wie meine eigene Seele. Ach! dass bisschen Verstand, das einer haben mag, kommt wenig oder gar nicht in Anschlag, wenn Leidenschaft wüthet. Wie wird mir das Herz so voll! — Das letzte Mal, das wir zusammen waren, gingen wir aus einander ohne einander verstanden zu haben: denn 'auf dieser Welt keiner leicht den andern versteht.'[2] Und dass ist gar zu traurig.

I pray you, thank her for remembering Victor Hugo's 'Songs of the Gloaming'; which came safely last evening, and which I

---

[1] Cf. *Hyperion*, I, III. *Ragnar Lodbroks-Saga* (edited by von der Hagen, 1828), acquired by L. in Heidelberg.

[2] *Werther.*

have been reading to-day. Also do me the favor to send the accompanying note to Mrs. W. A[ppleton] whose *fête* I shall not have the pleasure of attending.

> Good night, *liebes Fräulein*,
> Very sincerely yr. friend,
> H. W. L.

Sunday eve,
Dec. 10 [1837].

While waiting for his duties to begin, Longfellow worked hard on his lectures on German literature which were to be given in the third term. He also wrote a discreetly guarded letter to Fanny Appleton on January 8, 1837 — not of a nature to invite 'Damnation!' A proposed 'German Anthology' was rejected by Boston publishers.

Many of the students were immature: Edward Everett Hale entered Harvard in 1835, at the age of thirteen. He asserted, in later years, that 'little was done by tutors and professors except setting lessons and exercises, and hearing or receiving them.' [1]

From the beginning, the professor had his trials with the four foreign instructors, 'all pulling the wrong way, except one.' The undergraduates regarded these outlandish aliens as more or less a joke. It was a part of Longfellow's duties to look in on recitations, and virtually to conduct them, which young Hale viewed with delight. 'Spent the forenoon in hearing the German classes. I get much interested whenever I go, and must go oftener.' [2] In the third term (April 26, 1837), he took over the full teaching of a section in elementary German, which Hale attended:

> The regular recitation-rooms of the college were all in use, and we met him in a sort of parlor, carpeted, hung with pictures, and otherwise handsomely furnished, which was, I believe,

[1] *Life of E. E. Hale*, I, 19.
[2] L.'s diary of May 11, 1838.

called 'the Corporation Room.' We sat round a mahogany
table, which was reported to be meant for the dinners of the
Fellows; and the whole affair had the aspect of a friendly gathering in a private house, in which the study of German was the
amusement of the occasion. He began with familiar ballads, —
read them to us, and made us read them to him. Of course, we
soon committed them to memory without meaning to, and I
think this was probably part of his theory. At the same time we
were learning the paradigms by rote.

— a pedagogic method that squares with the most enlight-
ened modern practices.

In his boyish diary,[1] Hale remarked of this first recitation:
'The recitation, or rather the exercise, for we had no lesson
set before, was very easy. I think we shall like the study very
much.'

In his first summer-term, the initial series of Public
Lectures was given, twice a week, beginning May 23, 1837.
They were delivered from notes, 'without embarrassment of
the speaker, and to an attentive audience.' The seniors were
required to attend, members of the Law and Divinity Schools
were admitted. The first six lectures covered various Romance and Germanic periods; there followed a Sketch of
German Literature (1), Goethe (3), and Jean Paul (2).[2] In
Craigie House there is a considerable cluster of various notes
to lectures on German literature, undated, some of which
seem to belong to this course. I am inclined to place at least
two of these sets of lecture memoranda here: a) eighteen
small pages of 'A Sketch of German Literature'; b) the
lecture on Matthisson. The 'Sketch' begins with a translation from Menzel's *German Literature* (Stuttgart, 1828),
satirizing the 'bookishness' of the Germans. There are four
pages of a rather astounding attempt at a translation of the
original *Hildebrandslied*; also lists of chief works from the

[1] MS.   [2] *Life*, I, 261.

seventh to the seventeenth century. The lecture on Matthisson (who was by temperament closely akin to the American poet) is one of Longfellow's best characterizations. A number of original metrical versions from the Swiss poet were included: an unfinished penciled translation of *Adelaide*; the third stanza of *Die Vollendung*:

> Haste, oh haste! to wing my footsteps upward,
> Where beneath me sweeps this world of pain;
> Where in living fountains palms are mirrored,
> Where the dear beloved ones meet again.

The long *Elegie in den Ruinen* is reprinted in the Cambridge edition; *Der Frühlingsabend* has not been preserved. Of chief interest is the smooth translation of fourteen and a half of the original twenty-seven stanzas of Matthisson's *Kinderjahre*, in truth, a sweet poem! The similarity of this to Longfellow's *Lost Youth* (1855) is apparent in such a stanza as:

> I see the village willow-trees,
> And the meadow-brook below,
> Where the first thrill of joy I felt,
> And the first pang of wo.
> The place where under the blossomed may,
> On the white-blooming ground,
> To the merry music of rustic pipes
> The moonlight dance went round.

This translation is dated, 'January 2, 1837' — which strengthens the inference that the lecture belongs to the first course. Longfellow emphasizes Matthisson's melancholy tone, as of one cherishing a secret sorrow; 'he walks with the departed; his tone is soothing, like the cool of twilight. He loves nature, and the memories of childhood; he is not sublime, but beautiful. There is little strength — all is gracefulness and ease.'

With the close of August, 1837, came the beginning of a new academic year. During the summer vacation, Longfellow had rented two large rooms in Craigie House — which was destined to remain his fitting home until his death. The young professor's duties were more accurately defined: he was to give one oral lecture a week; to superintend studies and instructors, being present at least once a month in each course; to give two lectures a week during the summer term on 'Belles Lettres, or Literary History.' He determined to begin lectures on Goethe's *Faust* in the first term, and opened the course on September 18, 1837, speaking from notes, and giving two lectures a week — for good measure. The first lectures had to be held in a dining-hall, until another room could be fitted up. Young Hale was constrained to attend from the first, and commented, with the security of a fifteen-year-old Junior: [1]

> The lectures are to be extemporaneous translations of the German with explanations; as he called it, recitations in which he recites and we hear. He made a long introduction to the matter in hand, very flowery and bombastical indeed, which appeared to me very much out of taste. I believe, however, that it was entirely extemporaneous and that he was carried away by the current of his thoughts. In fact, he appeared to say just what came uppermost. The regular translation and explanation part of the lecture was very good.

Four days later, he 'went to Prof. Longfellow's second lecture, which I liked a good deal better than the first.' On October 27 the last lecture on the First Part of *Faust* was given. A volunteer section continued the Second Part. 'I shall not go,' states Hale; 'the lectures are tolerably interesting, but not enough so to compensate for the time taken up by them.'

[1] MS. diary.

Longfellow's teaching copy of the First Part of *Faust*, interleaved, and full of notes, is preserved, and is signed: 'Henry W. Longfellow. 1837.' While the book doubtless has some deposits from later courses, it gives a fair idea of the method of approach. The 'Introductory Lecture' is fully sketched on the blank leaves, and covers most of the subjects that would be treated in the most modern discussions: the widespread prevalence of popular traditions, especially that of selling the soul to the Devil — illustrated by many instances; the historical Doctor Faust; the first Faust-book; the treatment of the legend in the drama, beginning with Marlowe; the puppet plays.

In the text, many illuminating literary parallels to single passages are cited — from Sanskrit, the Bible, Old English, Rabbinical literature, the Edda, legends of the saints, modern poetry in many languages. The poet has contributed, from his own researches, some original materials: to *das dreimal glühende Licht* (l. 1319) he offers a picture, from *Ancient Mysteries Described*, of a threefold candlestick, used in some churches of the middle ages; to the 'Pentagram' (l. 1396) he quotes from Holland's *Cruciana* the statement that this sign was employed all over Asia in ancient times as a charm against witchcraft, and that Bishop Kennet reports the opinion that if the sign were placed against the body, the angles would point to the places where Christ was wounded. He questionably derives '*Lass mich nun erst das Kind noch tränken*' (l. 4443) from the Spanish ballad of *Conde Alarcor*. *Im Sünderhemdchen* (l. 3569) gives opportunity for an independent parallel from the history of the town of York, Maine. A philological note to *ihre vorgeschriebne Reise* (l. 245) is characterized by good sense: 'How much better it would be to say in English "fore-written" than "prescribed"! Thus the language would be developed from itself — and not over-laid with foreign words.' *Dass er nicht mag eine Seele lieben* (1. 3490) leads to a quotation of Saint Theresa's definition of Satan: 'Poor wretch! He does not love.'

Many fragmentary metrical translations are scattered throughout the pages, including an uninspired version of the *König in Thule*. From *Wald und Höhle* (1. 3217 ff.) there is the extended rendition:

> Spirit sublime! Thou gavest me, gavest me all,
> Wherefore I prayed. O thou hast not in vain
> Turn'd unto me thy countenance in fire.
> Thou gavest me glorious Nature for a Kingdom,
> And power to feel and to enjoy her. Not
> Cold, wondering visitings allowest thou only,
> Thou dost vouchsafe to me in her deep breast
> As in the bosom of a friend to gaze.
> Thou leadest the series of all living things
> Before me, and dost teach to me my brothers
> In the still wood to know, in air and water.
> And when the storm i' the forest roars and creaks,
> The giant pine, dashing, the neighbor-boughs
> And neighbor-stems, all crushing, downward sweeps,
> And to its fall, dull, hollow th' mountain thunders!
> Then leadest thou me to shelter'd cavern, showest
> Me then unto myself, and in my breast
> Deep and mysterious wonders are reveal'd.
> And when the clear moon rises on my sight,
> With softening power above, then hover round me
> From walls of rock and from moist underwood
> Of a past world the silver shapes uprising,
> And soften the stern joys of contemplation.
>   That to the human race nought perfect falls,
> I now do feel. Thou gavest me, with this rapture,
> Which brings me near and nearer to the gods,
> This same companion, without whom already
> I cannot live, though he so cold and insolent
> In my own eyes degrades me, and to naught

With one articulate breath turns all thy gifts.
He in my breast a wild-fire ever fans
For that fair, beauteous image, always busy.
Thus reel I from desire unto enjoyment,
And in enjoyment languish for desire.

One or two idiomatic translations are worth noting:

Ja, wenn man's nicht ein Bisschen tiefer wüsste (l. 3051):
'*Yes, if I did not know a trick worth two of that!*'

and, *in allen Ehren* (l. 3052): 'honor bright!'

It is everywhere plain that the lecturer aimed at the pleasureable entertainment of his listeners — surely a legitimate enough object.

In the second term of 1837–1838, Longfellow's second academic year, he began his course on Dante [1] — referred to in the letter to Mary Appleton. Hale went to the introductory lecture: 'Much to my delight, he rather advised those who had not finished the Ital. course not to attend till next year, which advice I shall follow.' [2] For the third term, the ambitious professor had planned giving his public lectures in the college chapel, a proposal which the Corporation 'turned down' — to his intense chagrin. On May 2, 1838, he began his new course on 'Literature and the Literary Life' in University Hall, 3. The introductory lecture included a sketch of Homer. To judge from the lecture notes in Craigie House, German authors were particularly stressed. At any rate, we find considerable materials on Richter,[3] Life and Writings of (E. T. A.) Hoffmann,[4] Tieck, Engel,

[1] Begun January 15, 1838 (E. E. H.).
[2] MS. diary.
[3] Diary, June 25, 1838: 'Completed lecture on Jean Paul.'
[4] March 7, 1838: 'Finishing my lecture on Hoffmann's life and writings.'

German popular tales, and an unusually complete and finished lecture on Goethe.[1]

We may say of these lectures, in general, that they show Longfellow as a pioneer and prophet in the systematic presentation of German writers to the American public. His estimates, not usually profound, often showing an uneven distribution of emphasis, are his own, derived from firsthand acquaintance, and stripped of the misty or rhapsodic phrases of German critics; the style is spiced with sprightliness — and distinctly out of the run of conventional 'learned' lectures.

The expressed wish, in the lecture on Goethe, is 'to show you how Goethe, from a buoyant, cloud-capt youth, perfected himself, into a free, benignant, lofty-minded man.' For the study of Goethe's life, *Dichtung und Wahrheit* was the chief source — with some lack of proportionate stress; as in the too large space given to such characters as Hofrat Hüsgen, for instance, while 'Lili' is practically ignored. In connection with the earlier life is given the

WANDERER'S SONG IN A STORM

Whom thou desertest not, Genius,
Not the rain, not the storm
Breathes terror into his heart.
Whom thou desertest not, Genius,
Will meet the hail-storm,
With a song,
Like the Lark,
Thou, above there.

Whom thou desertest not, Genius,
Thou wilt raise over the miry-path
With fire-wings;

[1] June 7, 1838: 'Wrote a lecture on Goethe's character and works.' The lecture is partly on the backs of old letters, the date of one of these being 'June 13, 1838.'

Wander will he
As with feet of flowers.
Over Deucalion's deluge-slime
Slaying the Python — light, great,
Pythius Apollo.

Whom thou desertest not, Genius,
Thou wilt spread thy fleecy wings beneath him,
When on the cliff he sleeps,
Wilt cover him with guardian pinions
In the midnight gloom of groves.

Whom thou desertest not, Genius,
Thou wilt in the driving snow
Wrap about with warmth:
To this warmth come the Muses,
To this warmth come the Graces.

.   .   .   .

Hover around me, ye Muses!
Ye Graces!
That is Water, that is Earth,
And the Son of the Water and the Earth
Over whom I wander
Godlike.

Ye are pure, as the Heart of the Water,
Ye are pure, as the Marrow of the Earth,
Ye hover around me, and I hover
Over Water, over Earth,
Godlike.

'In 1786 he made a journey into Italy, where he remained
till 1789 [!]' — forms the entire discussion of this epoch-
making period.

In Goethe's development there are three periods: 1749–1776,
youthful passion, aspiring and desponding, indefinite longings;
1776–1786, fiery passion under control. Passion assumes the
form of strength; 1786–1832, classic repose: 'to stand like Atlas

in the Battle of the Giants.'[1] The last period is the important
one.

After giving Menzel's fierce verdict against Goethe, Longfellow records 'my *own* impressions':

Self-culture, Goethe's aim, *is* 'selfish.' He was never idle; he
was a seeker for truth — and every one who looks in [to the
bottom of the well] to seek for it, sees only the reflection of his
own face.'[2]

Being surrounded by worshippers, Goethe was naturally
egoistic. As a Philosopher, he beheld beauty in everything, and
God in everything. One must fulfil one's own destiny: 'Like a
star, without haste, but without rest.' Deep enjoyment of the
present succeeded the restlessness of youth. He was an observer,
not a participator, as shown in his epigram:[3]

Why so battleth the People and crieth? — Would find
itself victuals,
Children too would beget; feed on the best may
be had.

Mark in thy note-books, Traveller, this, and at home
go do likewise:
Farther reacheth no man, make he what stretching
he may.

And now tell me, young gentlemen, what do you think of it?
From your own experience in the world — is it not best to take
most things coolly? even in the hot blood of youth? Have you
never been in a troublesome community where a difficulty in the
parish seemed to announce the end of all things? Have you
never had the misfortune to know a fussy, indiscreet individual,
whose bread-and-butter enthusiasm almost made you fall on

[1] Claudian's *Gigantomachia*, 23-24.

[2] One recalls Lowell's familiar remark in his *Rousseau* (1867): 'All men who know
not where to look for truth save in the narrow well of self will find their own image
at the bottom, and mistake it for what they are seeking.' Lowell graduated from
Harvard in August, 1838; it is highly probable that he heard this lecture of Longfellow's.

[3] *Venetian Epigrams*, 10.

your knees and implore peace? Have you never seen persons who think the world in a desperate state; are at war with everything, and enjoy nothing, because the time is out of joint? — How calmly the philosopher stands amid all this and says: that the best way to reform the world is to do one's own duty, and not the duties of others. Let each one labor in his sphere!

After a defense of Goethe in religious matters, come the words:

I will now state my estimate of that character in the fewest possible words: This man, then, was a man of comprehensive and commanding intellect; of rich imagination; and strong, simple, healthy common sense. In character he was calm and dignified; of great gentleness and benignity in his judgment of other men; of great sensibility to all forms of beauty; and great love for all forms of truth.

Discussing Goethe's writings:

He looked upon all things as objects of Art. He realized, not idealized. The reflection of earth lies nearer us than that of Heaven. We take little thought of the moral impression: all we can require of the Artist is, not to choose immoral themes.

There is naturalness: no effort, no struggle for effect —

> Immer hab' ich nur geschrieben,
> Wie ich fühle, wie ich's mcine.

He always writes to the public, never *for* the public. He is *objective*, losing himself entirely in any object or character, identified with it — as in *Iphigenie* and *Goetz*; he is also *subjective*, portraying himself in his book — as do most moderns — as in *Faust* and *Werther*.[1]

We sense in this discourse a notable advance on the one-sided and intolerant opinions found in the Heidelberg diary of 1836.

The ensuing year proved very laborious, but was much

---

[1] Longfellow continued to lecture on *Faust* throughout his teaching-career. On May 27, 1851, having ended the First Part, he noted: 'I am more than ever struck with the greatness of this poem.'

alleviated by the arrival on the Cambridge scene, at the end
of August, 1838, of a young man, who proved by far the
best 'find' which the Smith Professor achieved during the
whole course of his responsibilities. Bernard Rölker, the
new 'instructer' in German, remained at his post for eighteen
years, with no change in rank, continuing his duties after
Longfellow's resignation. Throughout, he was one of his
superior's dearest and most faithful friends. The rest of the
younger tribe of assistants, some of them scions of foreign
nobility, had vexed Longfellow's gentle soul mightily, even
to the point of uttering the term 'asinine'; compared with
them, quicksilver may be regarded as static. Longfellow
seems to have had his attention directed to this candidate
by Miss Crowninshield. He addressed a letter to Dr. Charles
Follen, in New York; Follen informed him that Rölker was
twenty-five years of age, was born at Osnabrück, had attended the classical school there, and had spent a year at the
University of Bonn. On arriving in New York, the previous
year, he had begun to study in a lawyer's office, and was
acting as tutor in the family of Judge Jones. In July, 1838,
Longfellow made a trip to New York to interview the young
man, and, after taking breakfast with him at the Astor
House, completed the engagement, which was to be so
remunerative to all concerned. Young Rölker had a nature
of sunny friendliness, and represented German open-hearted-
ness and good-will at their best. He was grateful for all that
America had given him, and became the most ardent of
patriotic citizens. He had hardly begun to teach, when
Longfellow noted: 'R. does well: has a popular talent, and
is very much liked.' He was a highly accomplished musician,
and within a fortnight Longfellow had taken him to a brilliant musical party at the Cushings'; soon after, he was the
central figure at an evening at Dr. Beck's, where he led in

[63]

singing German songs. He became at once an intimate member of Longfellow's circle, the 'Young Faculty Meeting,' which included Felton and Peirce, and held its Socratic *gaudiola* on late Monday nights, after the decorous sessions of the Faculty, 'as such.' The singing of German songs, whist, and choice suppers were the order of these nights. Felton took him to an æsthetic tea in Boston. In 1841 William Wetmore Story made a pencil-portrait of Rölker, which has still an honored place in Craigie House. Two years after Longfellow's resignation, he gave up his instructorship, returned to New York, and became a successful lawyer. This removal was for him a 'breaking away from the Syren voice of social ease and enjoyment, which had held him spellbound for so many years.'

During the earlier years, Longfellow had no better friend, though the relations became less close after the establishment of the home, and the entrance of Charles Sumner into the first place in Longfellow's intimacy. But he never ceased to be a welcome guest in the household, a marked favorite with parents, children, and friends of the family; he seems to have been socially popular everywhere. He addressed him, in letters, as 'My dear Longfellow,' and was always remembered with first copies of the poet's works. In 1850, Longfellow took over his German classes while he made a short trip to his native Osnabrück, an experience which caused him to become a more vehemently devoted American than ever. A year later, he made a complete English translation of Goethe's *Wahlverwandtschaften*, and (in connection with the *Golden Legend*) prepared an excellent prose version of Hartmann von Aue's *Der arme Heinrich*. His fine 'German Reader' was long used in Harvard. Toward the end of the poet's professorship [1] (sixteen years after the beginning of

[1] March 5, 1854.

BERNARD RÖLKER
Drawn by William Wetmore Story, June 3, 1841

their acquaintance), Longfellow wrote in his diary: 'Rölker came to dinner. He is a thoroughly upright, truthful man — an honest man' — which is perhaps as high a tribute as anyone need covet. The intimacy continued after Longfellow's retirement, and a hearty correspondence was kept up during many following years. Just before Rölker removed to New York, we encounter him as guest in the Longfellows' summer home at Nahant, where he 'sang German songs for the family, while watching the rising moon.' In 1858, in a very cordial letter, Longfellow says: 'Your letter came like a hail in the dark from one ship to another at sea.' When the Civil War came, he took a passionate stand for what he termed 'our struggle — the people against a baronial aristocracy.'

So close a friendship, lasting through full thirty-seven years, deserves permanent record: it undoubtedly had a most potent influence in freshening and strengthening the poet's vital interest in the best things of Germany.

A semester system was instituted at the end of August, 1838, which continued almost to the end of Longfellow's service: twenty-weeks' term from the end of August; six-weeks' vacation from the middle of January to the end of February; twenty-weeks' term, from the beginning of March to the middle of July; six-weeks' vacation until the end of August — a highly symmetrical plan, if the rest of society's arrangements could only be adjusted to it!

The sanguine expectation of the young professor, in beginning his work, that he should 'have nothing to do but lecture,' was doomed to be shattered on the rocks of college administration. Rölker had arrived at the beginning of the first semester, but a Frenchman was still lacking, so Longfellow took the French class under his own charge — 'for the present.' As might have been foreseen, he had to carry *all* the French instruction throughout that year, and during the first half of the year following. He had 115 students to teach in French,[1] and 30 in German. At the beginning of 1839–1840, the Corporation voted flatly that there should be 'no increase in instructors in Modern Languages, and that the Smith Professor ought to continue to give all instruction required in the French language.'[2] The Smith Professor addressed a letter to the Corporation, showing how they 'were swerving from the original design of the Professorship.' Before the second semester began, the Corporation allowed a new French instructor, and on March 8, 1840, M. Anatole de Goy took on his duties, and proved satisfactory, but 'suddenly left for France' during his second semester.

Before the beginning of 1846–1847, the Italian instructor had been dismissed, and 'the instruction in Italian was given by the Smith Professor.' On September 11, 1846, Longfellow 'heard both the French and Italian classes to-day; eight in all';[3] on October 9 he had 'four hours consecutive teaching in college.' On November 5, 1846, a committee proposed that he keep the Italian classes, and that 'hereafter, when Mr. Sales goes, the Spanish be added also to his duties.'[4] The Smith Professor apparently carried on the Italian work until the second semester of 1852–1853, when Luigi Monti[5] entered the scene; for, beginning with the catalogue for 1849–1850, the Smith Professor is also 'Instructer in Italian.' For 1850–1851 he was doomed to 'seventy lectures,... which hang over me like a dark curtain.' On September 16, 1853, 'A day of hard work. Six hours in the lecture-room — like a schoolmaster!'

An episode of 1839 witnesses to the existence of what was perhaps the first Goethe Society on this continent. A crudely-

[1] Higginson, 115.   [2] *Life*, I, 341.   [3] MS. diary.
[4] *Life*, II, 62.   [5] The 'Sicilian' of the *Tales of a Wayside Inn*.

written letter, dated June 7, which was sent by the 'Goethean Literary Society of Marshall College,' Mercersburg, Pennsylvania, requested the poet to become an honorary member, and referred to his 'general devotedness to the interests of literature (and particularly to German Literature; [1] as we learn through our worthy member W. G. Clark [2] of Philadelphia).' Longfellow was gratified, and for at least a year entertained the idea of making a foot-tour among the German-Americans of Pennsylvania. In the course of time came (as was to be expected) an appeal from the members of the Goethean Literary Society for money assistance toward erecting and furnishing a hall. [3] While Longfellow was recuperating at Marienberg, Professor Felton received two letters from the same group, begging him to negotiate a Poem from their Honorary Member, on the theme, 'Let there be light!' as an adornment for one of the Society's 'exhibitions.' He felt justified in refusing the plea, in the interest of the long-suffering invalid.

[1] This was before the appearance of *Hyperion*.

[2] Twin brother of Lewis Gaylord Clark.

[3] The letter bears a beautiful die-stamp, larger than a silver dollar, with a fine profile head of Goethe, and the Greek device, 'Let there be light!' It was stated that the Society had been organized in 1835, was rapidly increasing, and had already a library of 1700 volumes.

CHAPTER VI

Hyperion

ON SEPTEMBER 13, 1838, the young professor's diary shows the first mention of a new work: 'Looked over my notes and papers for Hyperion. Long for leisure to begin once more.' On April 6, 1839, he wrote at the end of the manuscript:

> Libro finito isto
> Gratia reddatur Christo.

The book appeared early in August, and is the most important single document having to do with Longfellow's transmission of German culture to the American people.

This many-colored romance is hard to appraise, but its vital heart is the relation of the author to the 'dark ladie' of Book III, Chapter IX. A week before publication,[1] he wrote to his intimate friend, Greene: 'I have written a Romance during the last year, into which I have put my feelings, my hopes and sufferings for the last three years.... The book is a *reality*; not a shadow or a ghostly semblance of a book.' 'I have great faith in one's writing himself clear from a passion — giving vent to the pent up fire.'[2] *Hyperion* stands alone among the *simples aveux* of all literary histories of the heart.[3] There has been some discreet, but rather silly, beating about the bush in regard to the patent identity of Miss Frances Appleton and 'Mary Ashburton.' The entrance of the heroine in Interlachen (III, III); the avowal, 'he who had a soul to comprehend hers, must of necessity love her, and, having once loved her, could love no other woman for ever-

---

[1] MS. letter of July 23, 1839.
[2] To Same: January 2, 1840.
[3] Perhaps the nearest parallel is Heine's *Das Buch Le Grand* (1827).

more' (IV); the sketch-book with a drawing of Murten (V); the discussion of Uhland's verse (VI); the 'proud Hermione' who 'disdained the love of a poor student, whose only wealth was a magic lamp' (VIII) — are some of the items which are fully documented from personal records. The tentative printer's manuscript of 1838 makes the revelations even more apparent: the name first given the heroine was 'Sommeville' [qu.: 'Pomme-Ville'?]; 'her hair was dark, and her face very pale.' In the same manuscript she was re-baptized 'Estrella de Silva.' 'Her mother is a Spanish Lady from Cadiz,' says the bluff Berkley [originally 'Brown']; — 'domestic tobacco, with a Spanish wrapper.' 'Estrella' was tentatively corrected in several places to 'Frances' [!], and 'Florence'; the author then, with moderated, though noteworthy hardihood, changed the name consistently to 'Francisca' — but in the end settled on 'Mary Ashburton.' The cadence of this family name leaves little to conjecture, while 'Mary' was surely, under the circumstances, 'next thing' to sister Fanny. Just before the last paragraph of III, v, was originally inserted the outspoken passage: 'I know not what others may think, but in my opinion a young lady of twenty, who can sketch thus, should not show her sketches to a young man of thirty, who has a reverence for intellect, unless she means he shall fall in love with her!' Of course, he 'invested her with superlative charms,' such as the authorship of his own sketch of artist life in Rome. In the diary of the earlier Cambridge days, the object of all his hopes was consistently referred to, when encountered on the streets of Boston, as 'the stately dark ladie' (in *her* diary of the same days, he is referred to — not at all!). At the beginning of 1838, he makes full confession to Greene of his purpose to win; but later, in the same year, he writes him: 'The *Madonna Francesca* is all dead and buried.' Still later, he confides to his diary the entry

that 'as yet F. E. A. shows no signs of yielding' — none the
less, *his* flag is still nailed to the mast. 'We meet only by
accident. I have given up society *entirely:* and live alone
here, grim as Death, with only that one great thought in my
mind.... I do a great deal in College; and devote all my hours
to literature — morning, noon and night.' In January,
1839, Charles Sumner admonishes him from London: 'Be
earnest, and success will be yours.' During that year, he
made frequent visits at the Appleton home. 'I am as much
in love as ever.... The lady says she *will not!* I say she shall!
... I visit her; sometimes pass an evening alone with her.
But not one word is ever spoken on a certain topic.'[1] A few
days later, the rocket of *Hyperion* was fired: history is silent
as to any commotion it may have made in the Beacon Street
citadel. In 1840,[2] Mary Appleton (Mrs. Mackintosh) writes
to Longfellow in the friendliest vein, and sends him a little
purse. On the very next day: 'Met the stately dark ladie in
the street. I *looked* and *passed*, as Dante prescribes. It is
ended.' Not until April 13, 1843, did the tide turn: on that
evening, 'at the Nortons', in the corner window,' they met,
'after so long and tedious a separation, and began once more
to draw near unto each other.' On May 10, in response to a
note from Fanny, Longfellow walked to town, 'with my heart
full of gladness and my eyes full of tears.... Day forever
blessed, that ushered in this *Vita Nova* of happiness!' The
letter which Fanny wrote, soon after, to the sister of Longfellow's first wife [3] belongs forever in the list of the most
perfectly attuned utterances of fine feeling and nobility of
soul. They were married on July 13, 1843: Fanny's gift
to her husband was her European sketch-book, beautifully
bound, and inscribed, 'Mary Ashburton to Paul Flemming.'
But the motley book includes much more than this vol-

---

[1] July 23, 1839.   [2] April 23.   [3] Higginson, p. 175.

canic Wertherian 'release.' Distant voices seemed to say to
the poet, 'Look into thy Diary, and Write!' Very funny
are the profound theories of learned critics as to the reasons
which led Longfellow to invent this or that feature, when, in
fact, he put them down photographically, as he actually met
them. The travels are an ingenious fusion of four expeditions:
the journey escorting Miss Crowninshield up the Rhine in
December, 1835 (with a curious back-turn from Mayence
to Bingen, I, v); an excursion to Frankfort with Baron von
Ramm, Julie Hepp and Miss Crowninshield (April 10–14,
1836); a tour of the German baths with Mrs. Bryant, her
daughters, and Clara (June 11–19); and his own solitary
pilgrimage through South Germany, the Tyrol, and Switzerland (June 25 to August 20). Here the Swiss experiences
(which came last in his travels) are put first, and the real
order of travel from Stuttgart to the Tyrol is reversed. Persons and events step freely from the diary into the romance:
the 'Baron' corresponds to Baron Jacques von Ramm, a
German-speaking lord of landed estates in Russian Esthonia,
who also lived at the Himmelhahn *pension*, and took frequent
walks with the young American, during which they discussed
German literature.[1] The man from Bayreuth, 'with large,
intellectual eyes,' who 'knew Jean Paul,' actually held forth
at a Heidelberg hotel dinner on June 4, 1836. Longfellow
fell in with the refreshing Englishman, 'Mr. Berkley' (in
real life, 'Kinsley') on the trip from Salzburg to St. Gilgen,
July 3; the incidents as to the tub of cold water and the
Latin conversation are literal transcriptions of reality — no
less the visit to the sculptor, Dannecker.[2] A real Pole *did*

[1] The scene of their joyous reunion as old friends seems to go back to the meeting
with Preble in Göttingen.

[2] The only touch of fiction is Dannecker's invented remark: 'You have a German
name. Paul Flemming was one of our old poets.'

seduce a young lady in Heidelberg — though she was not
a German from Ilmenau; the studies of German literature,
'Mary's' sketch-book, the witnessing of *Don Giovanni*, the
scenes in student life are likewise drawn from the journal.
It was on July 5 that the poet copied the inscription at St.
Gilgen, which makes the motto of *Hyperion*:

> Blicke nicht trauernd in die Vergangenheit, sie
> kommt nicht wieder.
> Nütze weise die Gegenwart, sie ist dein.
> Der düstern Zukunft geh ohne Furcht mit männlichem
> Sinne entgegen.

To traveling experiences are added the fruits of the intense
reading in which Longfellow immersed himself while in
Heidelberg — not to ignore his continued studies at Cambridge. The most obvious influence is that of Jean Paul.[1]
'The Only-One' means, of course, not the only writer worthy
of consideration, but 'the only one of his kind.' It was natural that Longfellow was arrested by this chaotic stream-of-
consciousness style, which present-day taste in romance will
assuredly not reckon as perverse: his enthusiasm was a
laudable 'revolt of youth' against the bland urbanity of
his earlier model, Irving — nor is the result without beauty
of imagination, eloquent periods, quick witty turns, and
sharp thrusts. At no later time does our author show such
devotion to this master; from the teeming chaos of Richter's
works, he selects, as the most vital qualities: tenderness and
manliness; a love of nature; wild imagination and playful-
ness.

In our own day, Jean Paul is blamed for a lack of clear-cut
organization of materials, of significant forward-moving

[1] See O. Deiml's valuable dissertation (Erlangen, 1927): *Der Einfluss von Jean Paul auf Longfellows Prosastil.*

action; for a tendency to go to pieces in his absorption in passing moods. All this is highly characteristic of *Hyperion*: vague terms ('dim,' 'dusky,' 'romantic'); elegiac moralizing; rhetorical apostrophes to the characters and the reader; fanciful titles to chapters — suggest the Franconian model. To these must be added an intentional archaic flavor, the use of far-fetched quotations, and delectably quaint allusions to unheard-of authors and events.[1] Sudden turns and incongruous comparisons (so typical of Heine, as well) abound: 'golden tears, which men call stars'; 'a kind of red-morocco and burnt-cork sublimity'; 'she let the crucifix sink down into her bosom, as if it were an anchor she was letting down into her heart'; 'Richter's thoughts are like mummies, embalmed in spices'; 'This was a disappointment, which the baron pocketed with the letter'; 'to console his companion; a duty which he performed like an old Spanish Matadora, a woman whose business was to attend the sick, and put her elbow into the stomach of the dying to shorten their agony'; 'took to himself many bad habits and a Polish wife.' (This feature is essentially vicious — or wholly delightful, according to your own temperament — far be it from me to prejudice anybody.)

The main tendency of the romance (as far as one may properly speak of any single 'tendency'), as well as the discourse on the life of the artist, plainly suggest Goethe's *Wilhelm Meister* (from which there is one direct quotation). The abounding lighter touches of irony may owe somewhat to Heine — possibly also the chapter 'The Landlady's Daughter,' which has some resemblance to an episode in the *Harzreise*. The chapter 'Homunculus' suggests wide studies

---

[1] Influence of Novalis' *Heinrich von Ofterdingen* may also be suspected: Longfellow read this romance with Clara in January, 1836, and remarked: 'Wild and singular. It pleases me — and strangely beautiful thoughts peep out.' Cf. *Hyp.* II, IX.

in the general field of the Faust-legend — not a copying from Goethe. The contempt expressed for Eckermann's *Gespräche* does slight justice to that priceless memorial.

Apart from these German influences upon the entire work, it claims a unique place in calling the attention of the American public [1] to a large number of notable German writers (not less than twenty-five), who are cited throughout the work. This is apart from the catalogue of the author's Heidelberg studies (end of Book I), or his allusions to Old English and Old Scandinavian sources. There are included writers of poetry, fiction, biography, literary criticism, and philosophy. Jean Paul, Hoffmann, Goethe and Uhland take the most important place. [2]

A full chapter on Goethe was entitled in the earlier editions 'Old Humbug' (the epithet derives from German critics). While not notably profound, this chapter may rank among the earliest American surveys of Goethe's totality, [3] and is a creditable summing-up of the poet's development, philosophy of life, and final significance: a 'glorious specimen of a man'; a 'realizer,' rather than an 'idealist.' Nearly one-half of the chapter was taken directly from the Harvard lecture of June, 1838.

Scattered throughout the story are a number of the author's translations of German lyrics — each one a faultless reproduction, in form and content, of its original: Uhland's *Der schwarze Ritter*, and *Das Schloss am Meer*; Schreiber's [4] *An die Glocke*; the folk-song, *Hüt du dich*; Salis-Seewis' *Ins stille Land*; the nonsensical student song, *Fuchslied* (in

---

[1] Up to March 31, 1857, 14,550 copies of *Hyperion* had been sold in this country alone (*Life*, II, 329). Unfortunately, the book is now out of print.

[2] In Appendix B is given a systematic list of German authors known to the poet.

[3] Everett, 1817; Bancroft, 1824; Felton, 1830.

[4] The 'Swiss poet' — actually, a devoted son of Baden.

twenty stanzas), and Goethe's *Ueber allen Gipfeln* (inferior to Longfellow's version of 1870). In the translations from Wilhelm Müller, Longfellow gave this much-beloved poet his first introduction to the English-speaking world. The version of *Wohin?* captures the airy freedom and lively movement of the original; the word-play of:

> Du hast mit deinem Rauschen
> Mir ganz berauscht den Sinn

is *almost* reproduced in:

> Thou hast, with thy soft murmur
> Murmured my senses away.

There are fragmentary metrical translations from Goethe's *Fischer* and *Wer nie sein Brot*; Matthisson's *Die Sterbende*, various *Volkslieder*, Müller's *Abendreihn*, Schiller's *Wallenstein*, and Luther's *Feste Burg*. The version of Hoffmann's *Kreisler* (IV, iv) is a model of sprightly translation — almost fully accurate. Finally, there is evidence all through the book that Longfellow had drunk deep from the fountain of the German *Volkslied*. Among his prized Heidelberg acquisitions was a fine copy of *Des Knaben Wunderhorn*; he also owned (and made enthusiastic use of) Erlach's large collection, *Die Volkslieder der Deutschen*, in five large volumes, and acquired Meinert's *Alte teutsche Volkslieder*.

No small part of *Hyperion* is derived from the Public Lectures on German Literature given at Harvard in 1837 and 1838. The young professor had spared no pains in the preparation of these discourses, in order to make them sprightly, brilliant, and captivating to intelligent listeners; he had put all his wealth of varied acquisitions into their substance and embellishment — and doubtless craved a more mature audience than that of fifteen-year-old undergraduates who found the lectures 'very flowery and bombastical indeed.'[1] Marginal notes on the original lecture sheets show how he went to work to adapt them for insertion in the romance. The chapter on Hoffmann (IV, III) has such an origin; even the epigrammatic 'He took to himself many bad habits and a Polish wife' had been earlier offered to the Harvard students. 'Jean Paul, the Only-One' (I, v) contains, in addition to many direct transcriptions from the Heidelberg diary, a number of literal passages from the lectures; one-half of the tribute to Goethe is copied directly from the Harvard lecture of June, 1838. The manuscript of the lecture on 'German Popular Tales and Traditions' has marginal notes which show that this, too, was intended to do its part in *Hyperion*.

Throughout the book there are countless whimsical turns of German idiom ('pickle-herring farces,' 'God's Acre,' 'under four eyes,' 'her blessed man,' 'Thou dear Heaven,' 'asleep in the feathers,' 'the only-one' — and the like), which show how completely the author had sunk himself into German patterns of thought while in Heidelberg. The passages on dandyism, and those alluding to Craigie House have, of course, to do with the early life in Cambridge.

In short, this rather undigested *mélange* has little organic consistency, and its outlines are strangely blurred: not on this wise does one fashion a concinnate masterpiece of perfected art. The writer served *all* that his ice-box contained — even a long printed clipping (the passage on the 'domesticated husband' in IV, II), cut from some magazine, enters into the printer's manuscript,[2] and makes one-fourth of the chapter.

An ample harvest for the half-year in Heidelberg: never

---

[1] E. E. Hale: MS. diary.

[2] It seems to be part of an unnoticed prose article which Longfellow had already published.

before had the American and English peoples been given so varied a panorama of German life and thought in the form of a romance. The literary judgments are fair, illuminating, and sympathetic, without any trace of servile worship of German influence, or a narrow condemnation of an un-American civilization; the 'gushing brooklet' of German sentimentality never quite 'murmurs his senses away.' A statement concerning 'Paul Flemming' lacks nothing in the way of lucid discrimination: 'underneath the flowers and green sward of poetry,... there lay a strong and healthy soil of common sense.' The New England inhibitions, which continually crop out, are expressed with the kindliest tolerance — as in the analysis of the character of the gay Baron, who, in spite of a world-wide difference in background, remained Longfellow's good friend: 'By the power of imagination, in him, the bearded goat was changed to a bright Capricornus: — no longer an animal on earth, but a constellation in heaven.' New England 'propriety' must have induced Longfellow to suppress the fairly discreet manuscript passage (following the remark 'Emma of Ilmenau was dead'): 'and that in her death two beings perished.' [1] The light touches of genial satire on German peculiarities (the absurdities of the Master-Singers; fashionable salons; grotesque and pompous student-fooleries) are keen and telling. The parody of philosophers ('Glimpses into Cloud Land,' II, VI) is not vastly inferior to Thomas Mann's pleasantries in the *Zauberberg*. It was a fair blow to deep-rooted Anglo-Saxon prejudices, when German 'brown papers, filled with greasy cakes and slices of bacon' were convincingly shown to be compatible with 'a glorious world of poetry, romance, and dreams.'

As late as 1852, Washington Irving, expressing admiration

[1] Cf. *Faust*, l. 3549.

for all of Longfellow's works, gave the palm to *Hyperion*. Freiligrath admired its brilliant and thoughtful presentation of German conditions — 'so different from those in America'; many years later, Agassiz praised the description of the Rhone glacier. While not adapted to the naïve enjoyment of analphabetes, it remains readable, and we may share, without apologies, the opinion of its writer, 'It will take a great deal of persuasion to convince me that the book is not good.' [1] In spite of all the sweepings which it contains, the work is essentially original; it had, for its day, a rich flavor of exotic adventure; its whimsicality and darting play of fancy remain engaging; its condensed humor is distinctly neat; its light irony (which could even touch felicitously upon the elemental passion for 'Mary Ashburton') — all this is delightful. The discourse on 'Literary Fame' is serenely prophetic, and elementally noble: 'It is better, therefore, that men... should be constantly and quietly at work, each in his sphere, regardless of effects, and leaving their fame to take care of itself.'

The book, like *Wilhelm Meister*, has to do with the progress of a soul. On revisiting Auteuil in 1836, Longfellow wrote: 'I was not happy then — I was too young and feverish: never satisfied with the present — and reaching out my hands to grasp the future, as a child tries to grasp a star.' To his friend Greene he wrote,[2] not long after the publication of *Hyperion*: 'My mind was morbid. I have portrayed it all in the book; and how a man is to come out of it; not by shooting himself like Werther; but in a better way.... Felton has given a fine indication of it as a Romance, though he does not touch this point, which is *the* point. If I had called the Book "Heart's Ease, or the Cure of a Morbid Mind," it

[1] *Life*, I, 337.
[2] MS. letter of January 2, 1840.

would have been better understood.' Mr. Lewisohn's thesis, that 'the self-revelatory and self-justificatory urge is at the core of all powerful and important literature,' would indicate that this work may claim a high place in the history of American letters.

CHAPTER VII

Life in Cambridge — Third European Trip

MERITORIOUS as Longfellow's services undoubtedly were in promoting an interest in German studies, it will not be claimed that he became a towering specialist in this field: the diverse demands upon his time effectually prevented that. For the whole summer of 1843 his eyes were almost useless, and during most of his later career were unequal to normal demands. By his unfailing kindly interest in the personal problems of unfortunates, he 'got himself in' with a host of persistent dependents. There was, for example, a desperate starveling of a young Irish poet, who bombarded him with incessant appeals, and *never* let go. A Polish count, with 'a fifty-Ogre power of devouring time,' invaded Craigie House for years. Professor Felton touched, with characteristic sprightliness, on such a personage in a letter to his colleague (August 5, 1851): 'He is the author of an English grammar which explains correctly the indicative first future. Theoretically, therefore, he has a just appreciation of time; but he does slightly underestimate the value of other people's time.'

The Smith Professor was beset by demands to furnish musical, literary, or scholastic careers for a host of Germans, Italians, and what not; Dr. Bosworth laid on him the burden of 'promoting' his Anglo-Saxon Dictionary in America; the poet Freiligrath looked to him to establish himself and his family in the Land of the Free. There were requests for honorary degrees, invitations (not connected with any remuneration) to write songs or odes for student societies, hymns for church dedications, English versions for alien poets; endless appeals for charity, and for autographed copies of his books for the libraries of obscure colleges. A stranger asked him to write a valentine, in answer to one he had received a year before from a young lady. He was expected to get up concerts and lectures for invading foreign 'talent,' and subscriptions for European monuments. 'College takes half the time; and other people with their interminable letters, and poems, and requests and demands, take the rest. I have hardly a moment to think of my own writings' (October, 1846). In face of the deluge of exigent letters, the long-suffering victim complained in his diary: 'Good people — sweet people! have mercy!' But he cannot be accused of neglect of his professional responsibilities. He did a prodigious amount of general reading in European languages. He clearly saw through the superficiality of much of the current fashion of discussing German literature and German philosophy. The Department flourished and grew. At the beginning of 1841–1842, when the work was very heavy, he was 'not sorry the new term has begun.' He served on an important faculty committee charged with drawing up a more liberal elective system; much earlier, he had an interested conference with Professor Felton on remodeling the college course. In 1846, the public German examinations were 'the best of all, as is usually the case.'

He cherished many 'other interests,' in a fashion which is anathema among strict pedants. 'Perhaps the worst thing in a College Life is this having your mind constantly a playmate for boys — constantly adapting itself to them; instead of stretching out, and grappling with men's minds.' He shuddered at the prospect of becoming 'a fat mill-horse, grinding round with blinkers on.' While showing a kindly interest in students (even sinners), he reveals no intimations as to his doings in the classroom, or his methods of teaching. College students seem never to have been invited to his home, or made the recipients of any social attentions. On one occasion he remarks that his classes 'need no preparation.' The Perfect Professor, according to Gildersleeve, is one who has taken the perpetual vows of poverty, chastity, and obedience. Longfellow was no strict Benedictine: the sole entry in his journal for June 13, 1839, reads, 'Went to town expressly to dine with Dr. Howard. Drank *Vin de Grave*; a wine which I like exceedingly. I think it would be fine with oysters. Try it, as soon as may be.' Social distractions were inevitable, and continued to multiply. On arriving in New York for a short visit, he found six invitations to dinner, 'and I know not how many to parties and concerts.'

As early as September, 1839, he found himself exhausted with labors in college: 'This will not do!' Hawthorne urged him to give up these duties entirely. While he was recuperating at Marienberg, some old friends sent him an urgent invitation to visit them in Italy. He noted in his diary: 'The warm South gleams and glistens with all its fascinations; — and at home gleams — with all its students the college.' President Edward Everett found it necessary to stir him up, from time to time, in the matter of reporting examinations. When the long vacation of 1846 began, he uttered a sigh of relief: 'Off from my shoulders falls the Term, like a full and heavy knapsack.' Two years later: 'The mill begins to grind to-day. Every year it grows more wearisome.' 'I shall never overcome my fear of lecturing, and shall never try to overcome it. The game is not worth the candle.' A growing cynicism as to the worth-whileness of the collegiate system (reflected ironically in Lucifer's diatribe in *The Golden Legend*) rooted itself in his thought. 'Pardon me, O ye souls who, seeing education only from afar, speak of it in such glowing words.'[1] 'They have come to bring sons to college. Alas! poor fathers!'[2] In 1852: 'Ah, if I only grind out something that is really food and nourishment for the young minds about me.'

In 1850 he 'seriously thought of resigning' his professorship; 'this college work is like a great hand laid on all the strings of my lyre, stopping their vibrations. It must be taken off.' In 1851 he 'passed up' Commencement, and remained in Nahant. On February 16, 1854, he made a formal resignation of his professorship, which was finally accepted in September. 'I am now free! But there is a good deal of sadness in the feeling. This separating one's self from one's former life!'

In 1839, he was reading many of Goethe's shorter poems, and had frequent discussions with Felton as to the latter's translation of Menzel's *History of German Literature*, which he later reviewed. At the very end of this year, Longfellow's first book of independent verse appeared, under the title *Voices of the Night*. This small collection brought together the poems he considered worthy of publication — from his earliest efforts, on. It included ten translations from the German, six of which had already appeared in *Hyperion*. 'The Happiest Land' is a mild version of a mild original, which has not been identified. Tiedge's *Die Welle* is a compact, significant thing, admirably rendered. Stockmann's *Wie sie so sanft ruhn*, an unrhymed, 'graveyard' product, is quite in Longfellow's native vein. *The Bird and the Ship*, by the amiable poet, Wilhelm Müller (whom Longfellow discovered for English readers), is not one of that author's most significant poems, but a fresh and breezy thing, whose spirit has been perfectly caught. The sixth stanza of the

[1] Diary, April 3, 1848.   [2] *Id.*, 1850.

[83]

original, which has a faint suggestion of 'impropriety,' was omitted. It is strange that editors have overlooked an obvious error in the last stanza, where 'Poet and Printer' have had an unfortunate disagreement. It is morally impossible that Longfellow (whatever his limitations) could have rendered *Jubelgesang* by 'weary song.' Undoubtedly he wrote 'merry song,' which, in his sinuous chirography, could have easily been misread.[1]

The Prelude to this collection indicates a turning from the more idyllic themes of youth to the stern issues of human life — and this confession, exemplified in a number of these poems, has been not improperly linked to the deepening in the poet's nature through his German life and studies. The much-admired, much-reviled *Psalm of Life* was written in Cambridge on July 26, 1838, when the poet was manfully 'rallying from depression.' Far too much has been made of the dependence of this poem-sermon on Goethe (especially because he read it to his students at the close of a Goethe lecture): as far as the spirit of action, of progress and growth through each day's experiences is concerned, it does reflect Goethe's main thesis. The incidental quotation of the famous motto of Hippocrates, 'Art is long, life is short' (*Faust*, l. 558), offers no basis for a charge of plagiarism: Longfellow was acquainted with the original of this saying as early as October 1834 (as shown from 'The Journey into Italy' in *Outre-Mer*), long before he had ever lectured on *Faust*. John Morley thought that he discovered some connection between the *Psalm of Life* and Goethe's *Das Göttliche*. The first line of *The Reaper and the Flowers*, 'There is a Reaper, whose name is Death,' undoubtedly derives from the familiar *Volkslied*, 'Es ist ein Schmitter, der heisst Tod,' but the

---

[1] The form of the word 'merry,' in his manuscript of *The Children's Hour*, confirms this explanation.

delicate treatment of the theme is far removed from the style of German folk-poetry.

The poem *Flowers* opens with an allusion to Carové's *Story Without an End* which Longfellow read, with much appreciation, in Heidelberg on March 10, 1836. Samuel Longfellow finds in this poem 'a mystical tone quite new to the poet's verse, and which suggests a German influence, appearing then for the first time in our American literature.

At the end of January, 1840, the poet gave three lectures before the Mercantile Library Association in New York. The third of these was on Jean Paul, and 'went off very well.' At this time he received a romantic-retrospective letter, addressed to 'Lieber Wilhelm Meister,' from friend Julie Hepp in Heidelberg — full of moonshine, flowers, and nightingales, and doubtless evocative of older memories and influences. Charles Sumner had brought her a (German) letter from Longfellow, concerning which she said: 'Sie schreiben deutsch beinahe wie ein Deutscher.' We find records in the poet's diary of a large amount of serious reading in foreign literatures, though it is by no means confined to the German field. 'Everybody,' he records, 'now talks about German literature and German philosophy, as if they knew something of them.' He sent to Joseph G. Cogswell (an almost forgotten, but highly meritorious name in the history of American culture), the editor of the *New York Review*, his article on Felton's translation of Menzel's *History of German Literature*. This was politely refused because of Menzel's attack on German universities. Cogswell wrote: 'I contend for the *absolute* excellence of German universities on philosophic principles and still doubt of their suitableness for lands in which there has been no especial preparation for them. Menzel is unquestionably a man of high talents, but he is a one-sided, prejudiced fellow, and I cannot abide him

[85]

for his abuse of Goethe' — and so the review went to the *New World*.

During 1840 he wrote the comedy *The Spanish Student*, drawn from Spanish sources (published in the Spring of 1843), and described by himself as 'a beaker full of the warm South; no German fogs or Scandinavian sea-weed about it — but music, sunshine and odours manifold.' The only performance of this play on the stage was in a German version, by Carl Böttger of Dessau, given at the Court Theater in Dessau on January 28, 1855. The theater was burned on March 7, which *may* have been one reason for the omission of further performances. The lines

> I can remember still...
> As in a dream or in some former life,
> Gardens and palace walls

may be reminiscent of Goethe's *Mignon*, while Preciosa's 'And this from thee!' recalls a similar remark of Luise to Ferdinand in Schiller's *Kabale und Liebe*.

At the end of 1841, appeared the small second collection of verse, *Ballads and Other Poems*, described by a competent friend as 'a prodigious leap forward,' and containing some of Longfellow's best-beloved songs. 'I have broken ground in a new field; namely, ballads.' In these, the poet sought to reach the heart of the people by stirring narratives in the spirit of older English verse; his success was immediate. Two translations from the German were added: Uhland's *Das Glück von Edenhall* (suggested by his friend, Samuel Ward), and Pfizer's *Der Junggeselle*. The translation from Uhland was especially happy, retaining the identical rhyme thrice-repeated in each stanza. Ward had also asked him to translate Pfizer's poem, after the death of his own wife and child. The change of title to *Two Locks of Hair* must be considered distinctly felicitous.

In the same little volume was included a translation of Bishop Tegnér's long sermon in hexameter, *The Children of the Lord's Supper*. Longfellow's first attempt in this measure (the forty-four lines of *Frithiof's Homestead*, 1837) was also a translation from the same Swedish author. The new production, which was composed in a surprisingly short time, not only shows a mastery of Swedish, but marks a praiseworthy advance in technique, indicating an approach to the style of *Evangeline*. The Klopstockian ponderousness of certain parts of the original, as well as the lighter idyllic movements, are admirably reproduced.

Having been invited to contribute to *Graham's Magazine* in Philadelphia, the poet sent an article on 'Heinrich Heine,' which was published in March, 1842 (XX, 134–137). A former appreciation of this poet is found in the letter to Mary Appleton of December 10, 1837 (p. 50). In his early Harvard lecture on Goethe, he offered a translation of Heine's tribute (copied into *Hyperion*); likewise in a lecture on 'German Tales and Traditions' he gave a version of a considerable passage from the *Harzreise*, relative to German legends (So stillstehend ruhig auch... hinter'm Ofen). The marginal notes to this lecture (1837 or 1838) show that this passage was also 'worked up' for insertion in *Hyperion*, where it was to have stood after the remarks on Müller's '*Wohin?*'.

In the article, it is stated that Heine is the leader of that new school in Germany which is seeking to establish a religion of sensuality, and to build a palace of Pleasure on the ruins of the church — repeating 'that old folly of mankind, living without a God.' Follows some light irony about young ladies and young men in America who hold the thesis that 'nature must not be interfered with in any way' — but discussion of this matter is waived.

Heine's style abounds in vigor, wit, and brilliancy; he lacks taste and refinement. In recklessness, he resembles Byron; in sentimentality, Sterne [two straight flashes of insight]. There are given two admirable translations, from the *Harzreise* and the *Reise von München nach Genua.* The article ends:

> The minor poems of Heine, like most of his prose writings, are but a portrait of himself. The same melancholy tone — the same endless sigh — pervades them. Though they possess the highest lyric merit, they are for the most part fragmentary; — expressions of some momentary state of feeling — sudden ejaculations of pain or pleasure, of restlessness, impatience, regret, longing, love. They profess to be songs, and as songs must they be judged, and as German Songs. Then these imperfect expressions of feeling — these mere suggestions of thought — this 'luminous mist,' that half reveals, half hides the sense — this selection of topics from scenes of everyday life, and in fine this prevailing tone of sentimental sadness, will not seem affected, misplaced nor exaggerated. At the same time it must be confessed that the trivial and common-place recur too frequently in these songs. Here, likewise, as in the prose of Heine, the lofty aim is wanting; we listen in vain for the spirit-stirring note — for the word of power — for those ancestral melodies, which, amid the uproar of the world, breathe in our ears forevermore the voices of encouragement and warning. Heine is not sufficiently in earnest to be a great poet.

This surely is not merely a critique of Heine, but our poet's own Confession of Faith.

In 1836 Longfellow had declared, 'my element is cold water' — and six years thereafter he was to have abundant opportunity to exploit this tendency. On account of continued bad health, which even vigorous exercise in the open air failed to relieve, he requested from President Quincy leave of absence for six months, beginning with the first of May — which was readily accorded him. On April 27, 1842, just

after having paid his outstanding debts in full, he sailed for
Europe, and made his way to Dr. Schmitz's aristocratic
Water-Cure of Marienberg, a former convent for noble nuns,
at Boppard on the Rhine, where he arrived on the third of
June. There is sufficient evidence to make it most probable
that he was directed to this institution by his friend, Dr.
Wesselhoeft, a German physician living in Cambridge. Dr.
Wesselhoeft had provided him with an introduction to the
von Binzer family in Cologne, and, later, sent him a long
letter to Marienberg. Some sixty patients were undergoing
the very drastic treatment of the place, to which the new-
comer submitted himself with an almost religious enthusiasm. While the poet's chief diversion (during the hours
when he was freed from the hands of the sturdy bath-attend-
ants) was making foot-tours, with titled fellow-guests in the
gloriously picturesque region of the Rhine, his studious
exercises began on the third day, when he read poems of
Freiligrath, 'the most popular of the young poets.' His
usual walking-companion was Landrat Heuberger, whose
delightful home was at St. Goar, the nearest considerable
town up the Rhine. He was a widower, and the father of
three talented and sprightly daughters. Although a high
German official, he was a fellow of infinite jest, bubbling
over with fun. The enduring impression which Longfellow
made on him is amply attested by the letters he wrote to his
friend in Cambridge during later years. A year after Longfellow's stay he dispatched an enormous epistle (well-nigh a
book), witnessing to the fact that the memory and influence
of the American professor were still strong and potent in St.
Goar. As late as 1876, when his eyesight had failed, and he
was compelled to dictate the letter to a grandson, he gave
evidence that his ruling passion for persiflage was as strong as
ever.

[89]

As a close friend and near neighbor of Freiligrath, it was natural that he should take the alien poet, almost at the beginning of his stay, to call on a celebrated German colleague.[1]

Schmidt-Weissenfels accounted Freiligrath the most genuinely typical, the most significant and individual of all the popular poets of his period. Buchner, in 1882, called him 'the most important lyric poet of the last fifty years' (eulogists are not averse from superlatives). His collected poems had been published in 1838, and this volume registered his 'first method': he had not yet entered upon that stage of political poetry which was later to make him the herald (as well as the victim) of the revolutionary movement. A volcanic vigor, 'Tiefe, Frische, Kraft,' was his special endowment. At this period, his individuality lay in painting nature in remote, exotic scenes: 'setting a turban on his Germanic head' — as he himself expressed it. He delighted in savage regions, in dazzling and colorful descriptions. His fancy reached out to Arabia and the tropics, to medieval deeds of daring: 'Der Norden, ach! ist kalt und klug.' He had a keen romantic interest in America, as a land unspoiled by conventional 'culture.' At the same time, he was a most faithful interpreter of his own northern seacoasts and forests, which he rendered with microscopic pictorial detail. Throughout life he was 'ever a fighter,' a bold experimenter, breaking with servile adherence to custom; he showed astonishing technical skill in metrics, and delighted in daring rhymes and unusual words. Many years' apprenticeship in commercial business had given him a full command of French and English, and he holds first place among the Germans as a phenomenally versatile translator of foreign poetry. With all his yearnings

[1] Cf. Dr. Maria Appelmann's dissertation: *Longfellow's Beziehungen zu Freiligrath.* Münster, 1915.

to transcend 'civilization,' he was of the most solid domesticity and inexpugnable private virtue; jovial, hearty, brave, highminded, affectionate, full of the joy of living, childlike in the sweetness and simplicity of his nature. Longfellow's first impression, at this time,[1] was clear and adequate:

> Freiligrath's poems are very fine. There is great vigor and freshness, and abundance of expression in them. His imagination is powerful; and revels in distant and almost unknown scenes; — the desert, the jungle; the lonely caravan — the negro, the lion. His subjects are almost invariably striking if not strange; and his metre and rhymes equally so.

Freiligrath and his sterling wife were living in rooms overlooking the Rhine at St. Goar; ideal harmony reigned in the home. The diary for July 14 has the entry: 'The Freiligraths are a very affectionate couple. I am delighted to see it. Long may they live to love!' The nearer circle of his friends, upon whom Longfellow made a deep and lasting impression, included (off and on) many of the most noted names in German literature. During this summer, Louise von Gall, a poetess from Darmstadt (who was also a wonderful singer, and at times entitled 'die Nachtigall'), a young woman of heroic, Kriemhild-figure and winning personality, was making her home under the same roof. She was, in addition, a successful writer of short stories, two of which she sent to Longfellow on August 24. A spirit of wholesome fun was atmospheric: the whole intercourse in the place was seasoned with delightful wit and humor. The owner of their apartments was named Ihl, and from that was coined the house-name 'Ihlium.' By easy derivation, Freiligrath was known as 'Hector'; his wife, Ida, as 'Andromache'; Fräulein von Gall became 'Helena' (or 'Gallina'), and the American (three years older than his German colleague) was adopted

[1] MS. diary.

into the circle as 'Nestor'; the baths of Marienberg becoming 'Pylos.'

'The friendship grew daily: the two poets valued and loved each other increasingly,' recorded 'Andromache.' The playful intimacy in their correspondence (which was to last throughout life) never abated. During the Marienberg period there was a constant interchange of books and visits, and a continued succession of happy excursions.

Testimonies from various actors in the scene of the first visit, on June 12, 1842, give a clear picture: Longfellow was first taken to the home by Heuberger. He was dressed in white, and presented a cool, vigorous, and distinguished appearance. After having dinner at the *Lilie* with Freiligrath, he returned. He informed Freiligrath that the latter's name was well known in the United States and England, whereupon Freiligrath pulled down an English Anthology from his shelves, and asked the visitor whether he was responsible for the poems printed under his name. The pleasurable assurance of being recognized in foreign parts was highly agreeable to both writers. Freiligrath enlarged on his special interest in English poetry, and Longfellow discoursed intimately on Dickens, Cooper, Irving, and other writers. He then handed his host copies of *Hyperion*, and *Ballads and Other Poems*. On returning home, Longfellow wrote: 'Freiligrath is a jovial, good fellow; and a poet of genius. Some of his poems are strikingly beautiful'; while Freiligrath communicated to *his* friends: 'He was exceedingly charming and agreeable.... Some of his poems are exceedingly good. He speaks German very well, and is a modest, amiable personality. As we are such near neighbors, I plan to keep up our association' — and in a letter [1] to the author, Levin Schücking (who later became the husband of Louise

[1] June 24, 1842.

von Gall), he described him as 'einen nicht nur *langen,*
sondern auch sehr prächtigen *Kerl.*' On June 27, Longfellow
recorded: 'I have read Freiligrath's poems in whole or in
part since I have been here.'

The voluminous and lifelong correspondence between the
two poets begins with a letter from Freiligrath,[1] dated June
22, written in beautifully regular *Frakturschrift* — would that
all Germans might follow his example! In this he thanks
Longfellow for his writings, which he at last has found
opportunity to read, and sends him two of his own publications. He admires Longfellow's intimate knowledge of Germany revealed in *Hyperion* (while reserving a full agreement
to his estimates), and informs him that he has already translated *Excelsior,*[2] from *Ballads and Other Poems.* Freiligrath
eventually made masterful versions of ten [3] of Longfellow's
songs, and translated *Hiawatha,* in full. Frau Ida and Louise
von Gall also rendered certain of his lyrics into German.
Freiligrath declared Longfellow's translations from the German (especially, *The Two Locks of Hair, The Castle by the
Sea,* and *The Luck of Edenhall*) to be among the happiest in
the English tongue — 'quite delicious.'

The month of July was filled with a cheerful round of
visits, dinners and excursions with the same group. On the
first day of that month, Freiligrath sent a letter, setting
forth the hindrances which had prevented him from returning Longfellow's visit, and enclosing his translation of *Excelsior.* He planned to add *Endymion, The Village Blacksmith,*
and *The Wreck of the Hesperus,* in which he admired the

---

[1] In Craigie House: unpublished.

[2] A later translation by Hunold aroused enormous enthusiasm among Innspruck
students.

[3] *Excelsior; Skeleton in Armor; Rainy Day; The Warning; Belfry of Bruges; Nuremberg; To an Old Danish Song-Book; Daylight and Moonlight; Vox Populi; Belisa-
rius.*

reflection of the tone of the old English ballads. Soon after, he sends an urgent letter inviting Longfellow to come to St. Goar, to meet his guest, William Howitt, the English poet. A letter of Longfellow's, of July 20, expresses the warmest thanks for his 'superb translation' of *The Skeleton in Armor*, and corrects the translation of a hard passage, which his friend had not understood. Replying immediately, Freiligrath sends a printed copy of *Excelsior*, from the *Morgenblatt* in Stuttgart, and encloses a long and most appreciative letter from Gustav Pfizer, the editor, who had also printed, along with *Excelsior*, Longfellow's translation of Pfizer's own *Der Junggesell* ('The Two Locks of Hair'), which Longfellow had made a year before. Pfizer had made and published, at an earlier date, a translation of Longfellow's juvenile poem, *The Indian Hunter*. In the letter, he expressed the warmest appreciation of Longfellow's rendering of his own poem, and urged him to come to him in Stuttgart — which is indicative of the widening of Longfellow's circle of German friends.

A four-days' trip down the Rhine had been arranged by the Freiligraths, and on July 25 Longfellow boarded the steamer which carried his friends, at Boppard. The group included Fräulein von Gall, and Justizrat Buchner and his wife, who had journeyed from Darmstadt to St. Goar, in order to take part in the outing. Farther downstream Professor Karl Simrock (poet, and incomparable translator of old-German verse) joined the party. The first night was spent at Rolandseck, where the famous ruin (which Freiligrath had once saved from demolition) was visited. The next day was given to the Seven Hills: landing at Königswinter, the expedition was augmented by Dr. Krah, mayor of that town, and his sister. The Drachenfels and Löwenburg were climbed, the ladies being carried by donkeys. To such a height did the hilarity of the occasion rise, that the learned Simrock could express himself only by throwing a series of summersaults on the grass — a gesture which the Harvard professor did not regard as edifying. When about to proceed to another stage, Fräulein von Gall was so content with resting, that she refused to rise. 'You seem to have caught the laziness of your donkey,' observed Freiligrath — to which she promptly replied, 'And you, its coarseness!' Longfellow disembarked at Bonn, to spend the night, and rejoined the party the next day in Cologne, where there was much sight-seeing, and other agreeable relaxation of the Spartan rules of the Water-Cure. On the following morning the whole group, much refreshed, took the steamer up the Rhine, to its respective abodes. Next day, Freiligrath sent three books relating to the Rhine, 'in memory of our excursion.' Other letters during this month point to a rapidly growing intimacy.

The severity of existence at Marienberg was tempered by an elaborate dance held in the institution on the thirtieth of July. Longfellow notes: 'Grand ball... very gay and swift-footed dancing.... We did not break up till half-past one.' The group at St. Goar was invited, but declined, on the ground of being fatigued by the Rhine trip; it is possible that the American guest was a member of the Committee, for Freiligrath's reply to the Committee's invitation is among the papers at Craigie House. Longfellow was expected at a cheerful Sunday party on the thirty-first at Heuberger's home in St. Goar, but preferred to rest, after the ball. At this party a group of young people gave a charade in honor of the American professor. A group of Fates spun a *long, long* cord, and commanded the Muses and Graces to twine it with flowers. For the second scene, two stalwart youths drank and bragged and boxed — conveying the German conception of 'fellow.' For the whole word, one of the same youths appeared as a short figure, which gradually grew in height — thereby also suggesting subtly the idea of 'Excelsior.'

Exceedingly broad hints (possibly more in accord with German than with New England taste) were distributed by the St. Goar group in regard to the American widower and the lovely Fräulein von Gall, but the visitor remained quite unshaken. At the end of July, Freiligrath, in writing to 'Nestor,' mentions 'Helena,' and adds: 'perhaps I ought rather to call you "Paris"!' Next day Heuberger wrote that 'die männerherzenerobernde Helena selbst dem alten Nestor noch gefährlich werden könnte,' and remarks later in the same letter that he had told her that if *he* were a woman, he would consider seriously becoming the Tenth Muse of a certain Poet. These intimations reached an incredible climax in a sonnet which Freiligrath sent the young lady, and which she had the saving tact to commit to the fire:

BRUDER JONATHAN

Du mehr als Stein! Kaltherziger Barbar!
Humaniorum nennst du dich Professor?
O Lug und Trug! Wir wissen's jetzo besser —
Ein Wilder bist du, des Gefühles bar!

Geh! eine Rothaut pack' am schwarzen Haar!
Skalpiere sie mit wohlgeschliffnem Messer!
Nimm dann ein Sitzbad, grauser Menschenfresser,
In deiner Heimat grausam Niagar!

Blut- Sitz- und Vollbad — *das* nur kann dir dienen!
Beweis: du sahst und liebtest nicht Gallinen!
Welch ein Verbrechen, Transatlantikus!

Wer das begehn kann — wo er immer wohne,
Er ist entmenscht, ist wild und ein Hurone;
Und nimmer rührt mich sein 'Excelsius.'

Even *after* Longfellow's marriage, Freiligrath and Heuberger rallied him for having disdained the German beauty. Fräulein von Gall was happily wedded to Levin Schücking on October 7, 1843. In that year, while she was living in Vienna, Longfellow gave 'Tom' Appleton, his brother-in-law, a letter of introduction to her at that place.

A major excursion to the lovely Wispertal was made on the fifth of August, on invitation of Adelheid von Stolterfoth, a meritorious poetess of that region, who was visiting the Freiligraths at the time. The group was entertained at the picturesque Kammermühle, 'with everything of the best.' In the evening, the party was rowed down the Rhine from Lorch to St. Goar. There was an indescribably gorgeous sunset, its golden glory enveloping the scene throughout the trip; songs and improvisations came spontaneously. The verses uttered by Freiligrath and Louise von Gall are preserved.[1] Longfellow's offering was as follows:

> To sail at eve with those we love,
> To mark the quiet waters flow; —
> The clouds like molten gold above,
> The stream like molten gold below.

Ten days later, when Longfellow's visits to St. Goar seemed too short and far-between to his friends, two humorous sonnets,[2] by Heuberger and Freiligrath, were dispatched down the Rhine. They were filled with comical reproaches for his slavery to the 'cure,' and abounded in clever and daring word-play.

The close friendship between Longfellow and Freiligrath grew and deepened during the ensuing years, and offers a noble record of unswerving fidelity: more than fifty of their letters (the majority of these are from Longfellow), extend-

[1] Ein Rhein-Idyll. *Deutsche Revue*, April, 1901.
[2] Texts in Appelmann, 24.

ing from 1842 until the last illness and death of Freiligrath
(March 18, 1876), are preserved. They reveal the heartiest
affection on both sides, and an intimate confidence which
extends to the most personal joys and sorrows. Only a few
days after leaving Marienberg, Longfellow sent back a fine
letter from Nuremberg, and another from London with a
copy of *Outre-Mer* and *Graham's Magazine* for September,
which contained the first act of *The Spanish Student*; at the
beginning of 1843, having resumed work at Harvard, Longfellow sent a very long and circumstantial letter, disclosing
the warmest personal feeling, telling of his doings in London
(where he passed a very agreeable fortnight with Dickens),
his return voyage, and his present occupations. The tone of
this correspondence grows in intimacy: from September,
1843, Freiligrath drops into the familiar 'Du,' while his
friend addresses him as 'Dearest Freiligrath,' 'Dearest Ferdinand,' and signs himself 'Ever affectionately thine.'
During all these years there is a constant interchange of
literary productions, a confiding of hopes and plans, a discussion of authors' problems. Longfellow sent various
gifts from time to time: Indian moccasins to Frau Ida, a
redstone pipe to her husband, a native basket to 'Helena,'
two of his portraits. In Marienberg Freiligrath had given
Longfellow an engraving of Schramm's picture of himself
(drawn from life in 1840), and this portrait Longfellow had
framed, and kept always hung in his study. Underneath it
was a painting of St. Goar, a gift from Heuberger.

Within a year from the time that the two friends had
parted, Freiligrath, who had always had a fine independence
of patronage or popularity, began that career as a political
singer which alienated so many of his closest friends (including Heuberger, Frau Schücking, and Simrock), and in 1846
drove him, with his family, into exile in London. There he

was forced to spend his days in the slavish drudgery of a small clerical position in a bank. Longfellow made untiring efforts to bring him and his family to make their permanent home in America: in 1847 he exhausted every means for having him made professor at Columbia, noting in his diary of November 27: 'He wants to leave smoky London and come here. Would with all my heart he could. But how to bring it about is the question.' Early in the next year he adds: 'Beck [1] and myself are making efforts to get Freiligrath here, and are trying to raise two thousand dollars.' This sum having been almost secured, to pay traveling expenses, detailed plans were made for receiving the aliens, with the intention of securing Freiligrath some suitable situation (as yet, quite undefined). Just as these plans seemed perfected, the March Revolution of 1848 broke out on the Continent, which caused the German poet to give a second place to all his personal concerns, and took him back in the same year to his native land, to bear his part in the *risorgimento*. As the world knows, that movement proved abortive; Longfellow learned on September 26, 1848, with much indignation, of Freiligrath's imprisonment, for a song against the King of Prussia, *The Dead to the Living*. For a second time (1851) the liberal poet was constrained to flee to London, where his lot became even harder. When Longfellow resigned his professorship in 1854, there was some possibility that Freiligrath might succeed to his place, though that was (happily) given to Lowell. Freiligrath's longing to become a citizen of 'the freest country in the world' had not abated, but the obstacles to his emigration seemed insuperable. In February, 1856, Longfellow sent him a generous check, in August another for twenty pounds; in May, 1867, one hundred dollars. He also contributed liberally to a general fund being

[1] Professor Charles Beck, the Harvard Latinist.

raised for his relief by Germans throughout the world. This fund reached the sum of nearly sixty thousand Taler, and enabled the exiles to remove to South Germany in 1868, where the poet lived in comfort, and highly honored, until the end of his days. Longfellow was making his last tour through Europe at this time, and wrote three times to his friend in an attempt to arrange a meeting — but Freiligrath's shifting from London to Cannstadt prevented this. While in England, he had completed a full version of *Der Sang von Hiawatha* (Stuttgart, 1857), with which Longfellow was highly satisfied. Shortly before his death, he wrote to one of his friends: 'Do you know Longfellow's noble poem, "Morituri Salutamus"? A melancholy, but courageous note of separation and farewell sounds through it, as also through many of his other poems. Dear, dear Longfellow!' He praised Longfellow's recent sonnet on Milton as *gross und gewaltig*. His daughter, Kate, wrote,[1] after his death, thanking Longfellow for 'his dear and comforting letter' to her mother.

> He carried about with him, all last winter, in the breast-pocket of his *Schlafrock*, the small volume of your poems, which you gave him at St. Goar, and which he often and often took out and smilingly showed to Mamma, saying invariably in a tender tone: 'Dear old Longfellow! Dear old friend!' After his death, my mother found in his private drawer, close to hand where he could always reach them (and they showed that they had been opened lately), a parcel of your early letters to him.... In one of the last numbers of last year, he brought in his magazine the picture of your library, which he admired extremely. Everything connected with you and yours gave him the keenest pleasure.

Professor Schanzenbach, of Cannstadt, wrote:

> A few days before his death... we talked of you... and his look kindled when he told me of the days spent with you on the

[1] Letter of October, 1876; in Craigie House.

Rhine and the long friendship he had entertained with you. One of his last writings was a translation from the *Masque of Pandora*. He showed me your portrait hanging on the wall.

A year after Freiligrath's death, on March 18, 1876, his American friend was invited to write a poem, to be read at a meeting in Stuttgart, which had been called for the purpose of raising funds for a monument. He sent a handsome money contribution for this purpose.

At the end of 1878, Freiligrath's widow wrote a long and admirable letter to Longfellow, thanking him for a recent communication; in the course of this letter she told of the recent celebration of Heuberger's eighty-ninth birthday, and added that he had intimated that the summer of 1842 had 'formed the most interesting episode in his long life.' The following recently-discovered letter to Freiligrath's daughter Kate may serve as a concluding document in the correspondence:

Dear Mrs. Kroeker,   CAMBRIDGE, *May* 30, 1880.

Please accept my sincere and cordial thanks for your kind remembrance, and for your two articles on the 'National Poetry of Servia.'

I have read them with great pleasure. The specimens you give are charming; and show that you have inherited your father's skill in translation.

That dear father! How much I lament his death! But he seems to be brought back again to me almost, now that his beloved books are in Boston. You will be glad to know that they are prized and cherished by the owner, and have a house and home worthy of them.[1] I rejoice that they have not been scattered to the four winds!

I beg you to remember me most kindly to your mother, when you write to her, and always to believe me,

Your faithful friend
HENRY W. LONGFELLOW

[1] They were bought by Mr. J. M. Sears, of Boston.

The ten translations which Freiligrath published are models in this difficult art. (Incidentally, *The Rainy Day* was done by his gifted wife.) While far from being the only versions which made the American poet known in Germany, they are incomparably the best. Another poetic tribute was offered by Freiligrath in a 'Toast,' delivered at Stuttgart on the fourth of July, 1870; addressing 'the host of German singers in America,' the last stanza reads:

> So wird es dir an Ruhm nicht mangeln;
> So, ebenbürtig, stellst du froh
> Dich einst zum Bruderchor der Angeln:
> Zu Bryant und zu Longfellow!
> Dem Pfade Heil, den du betreten!
> Wir grüssen dich, wir sind dir nah! —
> Das Glas gefüllt! Hoch die Poeten,
> Die deutschen, in Amerika!

As touching the literary influence of Freiligrath upon our American poet, there is not much to be recorded. The Germans, with the liberality which characterizes them in these matters, are inclined to regard this contact as epoch-making — which it assuredly was not. 'Longfellow,' we are told, 'follows him in the use of the desert, of sound-color, contrast-effects, clear delineation, dramatic liveliness, and colorful exotic rhymes.' The immediate working was practically confined to the *Poems on Slavery*, which Longfellow composed while lying seasick in his cabin on the *Great Western*, on the return journey. The *Slave's Dream* is undoubtedly connected with *Der Mohrenfürst*; Longfellow wrote on January 6, 1843: 'In the "Slave's Dream" I have borrowed one or two wild animals from your menagerie!' However, it is no servile imitation. The slave, who 'started in his sleep, and smiled,' has not much in common with the Moorish prince who battered his drumhead to pieces; while Longfellow's

'Eugene-Aram' meter gives an entirely different color to the whole picture.

The Witnesses, beginning:

> In Ocean's wide domains,
> Half buried in the sands,
> Lie skeletons in chains,
> With shackled feet and hands —

has striking similarities to *Die Toten im Meere*:

> Tief unter grüner Meereswell'
> Auf Muschelbank und Kies,
> Da schlummert mancher Schiffsgesell,
> Der frisch vom Lande stiess —

though its tendency is altogether different. Freiligrath's *Scipio* pictures a wealthy master, whose Creole maid is attired in a cochineal-colored garment, and possesses notable eyes, hair and mouth; Longfellow's *Quadroon Girl* also has large eyes, and wears a bright gown; her own father sells her into slavery.

Of later poems, *To The Driving Cloud*, like Freiligrath's *Negro on Skates*, concerns the contrast between a savage in his native environment and the same individual transported into modern surroundings. Longfellow's classical hexameters, however, lend a distinctly individual character. As to the intimate *To a Child*, we are told that 'the poet's fancy roves to distant scenes; he uses curious rhyme-words.' This is one of Longfellow's most personal poems: the oriental allusions are suggested directly by actual tiles in Craigie House. *Seaweed* and *Moos-Tee* have been linked — though two more dissimilar poems could not be cited.

In *The Day is Done*, the phrase 'like the Arabs' reminds a German scholar of Freiligrath's 'poetry of the desert.' Longfellow had used the phrase, 'Here, Arab-like, is pitched my tent,' in 1841, before he had any knowledge of Freiligrath. One must infer that the latter discovered the palmtree, and invented the camel. In short, all allusions to the tropics (concerning which an intelligent American scholar may be presumed to have had some information) are summarily accredited to the German model. Dr. Appelmann discovers that the idea of 'children, as living poems' was suggested by Freiligrath's letter of April 2, 1857; this allusion is merely a reflection from Longfellow's own letter of January 27 of that year; besides, the poem, *Children*, in which the familiar comparison originally occurs, was written on February 1, 1849! In fact, the two poets were temperamentally quite disparate: just after his return to Cambridge, Longfellow tried to translate some of his friend's poems, but 'found them too difficult.'

A few further matters in connection with the poet's third visit to Germany are in place:

The zeal which had led him to exploit every cultural opportunity to the full was somewhat tempered by the fact that his first aim on this trip was the recovery of his health. We find this entry in the Marienberg diary: '*Dolce pensar niente*. I have no time to note down my impressions, nor to work out the trains of thought that come into my mind. I should like to write some poems, but cannot. I must give the time up, as I intended, to physical education.' Longfellow's relaxation, however, would seem much like labor to other people: he compassed a large amount of reading in German literature, and recorded his impression of each work. Freiligrath's and Herwegh's poems, likewise those of Geibel, Lenau, Zedlitz, Auersperg, Immermann and Becker; Eberhard's *Hänchen und die Küchlein*; Dingelstedt's *Lieder eines Nachtwächters*; romances by König and Gutzkow; Frau von Binzer's story, *Die Verlobung*; Hackländer's *Bilder von dem*

Soldatenleben; the Volksbuch of *St. Genevieve*; Simrock's *Rheinsagen*; Schröter's *Finnische Runen*; the *Nibelungenlied* — all these were faithfully disposed of. A few weeks before leaving, he wrote (not for publication) the noble sonnet, *Mezzo cammin*: he had passed his thirty-fifth year, and up to this time had failed to achieve the ambition of his youth, 'to build some tower of song with lofty parapet.' Looking back on life, and pondering the inevitable end, he cherishes a hope of 'what I may accomplish yet.'

Longfellow had set great store on visiting the military maneuvers of some fifty thousand troops near Bonn: 'a bivouac and a night under a tent and the *reveillé* are things to make an impression upon one for evermore.' He urged Freiligrath to be his guest and companion. While refusing to accept the first offer, his friend hoped to join him — which Longfellow again begged of him in a very urgent letter. On further consideration, Freiligrath felt compelled to refuse: he had not attended the dedication of the Cologne Cathedral, and his appearance in a camp might be misinterpreted by his political enemies. He gave him, however, introductions to various officers, but warned him against disillusion. From September 10 to 12, Longfellow attended the affair, alone, stopping to call on Karl Simrock at Bonn — but the weather was bad, and, like the late Queen, he 'was not amused.'

The time for return to college duties was now at hand: a request for an extension of leave for a further year was answered in good-humored fashion by President Quincy: he regretted Longfellow's continued ill-health, but had secured the six-months' vacation with difficulty, and only on Longfellow's assurance that he would return in October. If he were to stay longer, the Senior class would have no opportunity to profit from his instruction. Another year in Europe

[105]

would be permitted, but the professor's salary would be discontinued at the end of November. Accepting the decree of fate, Longfellow dispatched a large box of books (German, Flemish, and French) which he had collected, and on September 18 took reluctant leave of Marienberg. His way led through Mainz, where he witnessed a convention of natural scientists. Going farther south, he traveled with one of them as far as Nuremberg, and explored the city with him. While on this trip, he copied into his diary (which is preserved) O. L. B. Wolff's *Der gute George Campbell*, which he found in Gollmich's *Deutscher Sänger-Saal* — not suspecting that it was a translation of a Scotch ballad, though he added the discriminating comment: 'The idea "And my child still unborn" is worthy of any of the old ballads.' This harmless incident was used by Poe as the ground for his most venomous charge of wilful plagiarism.

The feverish trailing after 'sources' (possibly illustrated by the present work) led to exaggerated charges of 'borrowing' on Longfellow's part. Unjust as they generally were, they wounded him to the center of his sensitive nature — but he refused to accord them the recognition of a public reply.[1] Only to the confidential pages of his private diary did he disclose the injustice of these attacks. After having written the line,

The houses hearsed with plumes of smoke,

he consulted a dictionary as to the use of the word 'hearsed,' and found a quotation from Crashaw (which he had never seen):

The house was hearsed about with trees.

[1] In 1879, he wrote to Greene: 'Only in one solitary instance, early in life, have I ever taken any notice of anything said of me in the newspapers.'

In the ode, *To a Child,* he spoke of

> The buried treasures of the miser, Time.

Five years afterward, in reading, for the first time, Wordsworth's ode, *On the Power of Sound,* he was startled on encountering,

> All treasures hoarded by the miser, Time.

Such coincidences would have been greedily seized upon by his traducers, if they had discerned them. A Washington newspaper, not versed in Longfellow's actual sources, boldly accused him of taking incidents from the *Kalevala,* and foisting them upon the public in *Hiawatha,* as legends of the American Indians. Freiligrath wrote, after the death of his son, 'Einsam, einsam, einsam in den Räumen,' etc.; Longfellow's words, 'Return from Nahant to this desolate, desolate house,' have been pointed out as a borrowing, though he set them down in his diary twelve years before the writing of Freiligrath's letter.

Morin,[1] in *Les Sources de l'Œuvre de Henry Wadsworth Longfellow,* Paris, 1913, points out that the eloquent apostrophe,

> Sail on, O Union, strong and great!

at the close of *The Building of the Ship,* shows the dependence of this poem on Schiller's *Bell,* which closes with a reference to 'Concordia.' He quite overlooks the fact that Longfellow's original conclusion was a pessimistic elegy on the passing of the proudest works of man, and that the stirring final passage was substituted in view of the threats of secession which were rocking the nation. It requires a more-than-German ingenuity to identify Schiller's vague 'harmony' with the

---

[1] The theory of a possible organic connection between this name and 'Moron' is undocumented and inadmissible.

[107]

political constitution of the United States of America. Another critic was convinced that the legend of 'Mondamin' was taken from Burns's 'John Barleycorn'! The sum of such repeated fatuities has naturally led to a certain degree of credence:

Gutta cavat lapidem, non vi, sed saepe cadendo.

Adolf Strodtmann, author of an exhaustive and exhausting life of Heine, stated in his *Amerikanische Anthologie* that 'Many of Longfellow's best productions disclose themselves as successful imitations of foreign poems — especially those of Heine, Uhland, Freiligrath, and Hugo.' It is of interest to add that *his* list of noteworthy American poets consists of C. P. Shiras, Dorgan, Piatt, Bradstreet, Hewitt, Embury, Sawyer, Oakes-Smith, Osgood, and Stuart Sterne.

On Longfellow's journey southward, a breezy young commercial traveler in the same coach shouted out a pat quotation from one of Freiligrath's poems — which greatly pleased his friend.

His keen delight in that most-German city, Nuremberg, is reflected in a hearty letter of September 24 from that place, addressed to the friends at St. Goar. The panorama of the city, its musical bells, its dialect, its thronging memories of art, history, and poetry found a full response in the poet's soul. Some years later, he sent to the same friends his poem *Nuremberg*, which so perfectly captures the quaint charm of the place, and the memory of times 'when Art was still religion'; and pays sympathetic tribute to 'the nobility of labor, — the long pedigree of toil.'

Returning northward, he reached St. Goar on September 29, and remained in the familiar home until the first of October. Kinkel, of Bonn, was also there as guest. On the last evening, the two friends paced to and fro along the Rhine until near midnight, and opened their deepest souls. Freiligrath accompanied the traveler on the steamer downstream as far as Coblenz, where, with glowing eyes, Longfellow clasped his hand and said: 'God bless you, God bless you, dear friend!' They were not to meet again.

CHAPTER VIII

Early Married Life — Academic Duties — Studies and
Publications

IN GENERAL, the poet's years moved on with much serenity,
and one may speak of a relative abatement of zeal in German
studies. At the time of his second marriage (July 13, 1843)
his eyesight had almost completely failed, but he had every
help from his gifted wife, who possessed an admirable knowledge of German, and was unwearied in lending her competent secretarial help. Her reading aloud was a supreme joy
to her husband, and enhanced the significance of all that she
interpreted. The Professor of Modern Languages by no
means confined his readings to any one European field.
Even before his marriage, he had begun the translation of
Dante's *Divine Comedy*, which was to occupy much of his
interest for many years, and was not completed until 1863.
We have record of German books purchased, including German lyric poets, and the Life and Poems of Körner. The
popularity of his lectures on *Faust* is shown from a letter from
President Quincy (March 15, 1844), asking him to change
the time of his lecture-hour, as 'many, if not all, of the
Juniors wish to attend them.' Just at this time the diary
records: 'In the evening Fanny — the divine Fanny — read
to me from the *Heldenbuch*' — including *Hugdietrich* and
Wolfdietrich. She also read him the *American Sketches* of
Sealsfield, in translation (Longfellow assumed that this
author was an American), Jean Paul's *Flegeljahre*, and
Fichte's *Life* (by Smith), as well as his lectures on *The
Nature of the Scholar*. The comment in the diary is: 'And this
is a German philosopher! Why, there is more of the soul of

Christianity in these lectures than in the sermons of all the
rebel crew of narrow-minded, dyspeptic, so-called *orthodox*
preachers who rail against German philosophy, should they
preach from one end of the year to the other!' On May 26,
1846: 'Home at eight, to the sweet smile of Fanny, sitting in
the lamp-light, with a book in her hand.' A few days later:
'Fanny sat under the linden-tree and read to me Heine's
poems.... Heine, delicious poet for such an hour! What a
charm there is about his *Buch der Lieder*! Ah, here they
would be held by most people as ridiculous. In truth it
must be spoken and recorded — this is a dreadful country for
a poet to live in. Lethal, deadly influences hang over him,
the very "Deadly Nightshade" of song. Many poetic souls
there are here, and many lovers of song; but life and its ways
and ends are prosaic in this country to the last degree.'

On June 8 and 11 were read the first two parts of Goethe's
Italiänische Reise: 'written in his usual lucid, simple style,
and resembling the conversation of an elegant and very
intelligent man, who has all his faculties of observation
keenly alive;... it is striking to read Dickens's Letters from
Italy in connection with Goethe on the same theme. One is
all drollery, the other all wisdom. They were of about the
same age when their journeys were made.' *Pegasus in Pound*
(published, 1846) has an unquestionable derivation from
Schiller's *Pegasus im Joche*.

In September, 1843, Carey and Hart, of Philadelphia,
had offered Longfellow one thousand dollars for the compila-
tion of an encyclopedic volume, *Poets and Poetry of Europe*,
and to this huge project he valiantly addressed himself,
gathering poetic translations (many of which were his own),
and writing the historical and critical introductions. The
collection represented some four hundred Continental poets.
Owing to the parlous condition of his eyesight, he summoned

Professor Felton to his aid, and shared with him labor and emolument. In March, 1844, 'having now begun with the German,' he wrote to his father, in Portland, asking that one of his brothers might copy all the translations of Freiligrath contained in the *Dublin University Magazine.* The bulky volume, having as its frontispiece a portrait of Schiller, was published in the summer of 1845; German poets, extending from the early centuries to contemporary times, were largely represented. Fourteen of these poems were in Longfellow's translation; seven of them, which first appeared in earlier volumes, have been already noticed. Those made especially for this work were: that evergreen *Volkslied, O, Tannenbaum*; the anonymous *Silent Love*, a pleasing little stanza (from *Gute Lehre*, in Ehrlach), faultlessly turned; Simon Dach's *Anke von Tharau*, which has become an authentic *Volkslied.* The last half of this conjugal lyric maintains the thesis that married life becomes a 'dog-and-cat' existence, unless the wife renders a complete subjection to her husband in all matters lying outside kitchen management. These rather practical stanzas are not found in countless popular collections which contain this poem, but Longfellow had the literary courage to translate them in full.[1] Dach's *Blessed are the Dead*, Mosen's *Statue over the Cathedral Door* and *Legend of the Cross-Bill*, and Heine's *The Sea hath its Pearls* (unrhymed) are rendered impeccably. A new edition of *Poets and Poetry*, with a supplement, appeared in 1871. Here Schiller's portrait was supplanted by that of Goethe, and there was an engraved title-page with a view of the Rhine. No new translations from Schiller were added, but Longfellow's beautiful versions of Goethe's two *Wanderer's Night-Songs*, and extracts from Bayard Taylor's translation of the Second Part of *Faust* were included. This may be

[1] He used Wilhelm Müller's popular texts for the translations from Dach.

symptomatic of the growing importance of Goethe in Longfellow's esteem.

In the collection, *The Belfry of Bruges*, published on December 23, 1845, there are a number of allusions to German imperial history (especially the doings of Maximilian I); the pleasing poem, *Walter von der Vogelweid*, is built about the legend of the feeding of the birds on his tomb, and refers to the *Wartburgkrieg*; in the sonnet *Autumn*, there is a felicitous allusion to the legend of Charlemagne's 'golden bridge' over the Rhine at Bingen.[1] The small volume contained, also, six translations from the German, five of which have been discussed in connection with *Poets and Poetry of Europe*. The only new offering was the group of twelve short 'Poetic Aphorisms' taken from that pungent and prolific epigrammatist, Friedrich von Logau, who flourished at the time of the Thirty Years' War. All of these were culled from Wilhelm Müller's *Poets of the Seventeenth Century*. Longfellow's version of 'Retribution,' in this group, has furnished, perhaps, the tritest quotation in the English language — though it is usually *mis*-quoted.

In 1846, Longfellow attended Emerson's lecture on Goethe; in 1847 he read from Ida von Hahn-Hahn's novel, *Ulrich*; in 1848 he read Gostwick's *Spirit of German Poetry*.

Evangeline was finished, after many interruptions and misgivings, on its author's fortieth birthday — at the *mezzo cammin* of his career. This exquisite thing had greater success than any earlier publications, and is the high-water mark of his achievement. Here, in 'the stateliest measure ever moulded by the lips of man,' the anointed Artist gave full proof of his calling. Its irresistible pathos and unaffected sweetness; its pure music (enhanced by melodious Indian words); its sustained interest; its richness of poetic material,

[1] From Geibel's *Die goldne Brücke*, in Simrock's *Rheinsagen*.

and its charm of phrasing and diction justify the affirmation of Longfellow's greatness. The incorruptible Freiligrath's immediate and highly competent verdict was (March 11, 1848):

> It is a masterpiece.... I cannot now enter into any details; but I cannot omit to mention how, among so many other beautiful passages, I was struck by that truly grand and sublime one, when the returning tide suddenly answers the voice of the priest at old Benedict's funeral service. Such strokes reveal the poet.

The work has a characteristic Catholic atmosphere which has led many Romanists to claim boldly our Puritan-Unitarian poet as one of their own.[1]

A few obvious resemblances to Goethe's *Hermann und Dorothea* have frequently been touched on — but here, as elsewhere, our German friends allow their constructive imagination to run well ahead of the facts. The names of Klopstock, Voss, and Goethe are forever associated with the modern revival of classical hexameter — *ergo*: *Evangeline* is a 'German' production. It is the old assumption, that because Longfellow revered and studied certain masters, he was a mere pupil, who sat meekly at their feet. The American poet called his work an 'idyl'; it has to do with the love of two young people, which encounters obstacles; the Muse is (once) invoked; there is a discussion of the political situation; a good parish priest appears; there is even mention of pipes and tobacco. Freiligrath set his copy on the shelf alongside *Hermann und Dorothea* — and here the resemblance ends. There is not one line which shows a sign of direct imitation.[2]

[1] Cf. A. Baumgartner, S. J.: *Longfellow's Dichtungen.* Freiburg, 1887.

[2] Possibly the word-order in II, 1:

> .... *before her* extended

> . . . . . .
> Marked by the graves of those who had sorrowed and suffered *before her*, may be a faint echo of *H. und D.*, II, 229–230; there is also 'the fruitful valley,' which *is* suggestive of *Dieses fruchtbaren Tals* (I, 12).

When one compares Goethe's liberal (and verbal) borrowings from *Luise,* the overstressed charge of 'imitation' falls to the ground. Longfellow knew and admired Goethe's work — though there is no record of his having studied it at the time when he was writing *Evangeline.* In 1838, he called it 'a very simple, singular, and beautiful poem, of a style to please Wordsworth.' In 1840, in inviting Sumner to Cambridge, he said: 'So make up your bundle, putting in "Esmeralda" and "Hermann und Dorothea."' Longfellow's poem has far more fancy, more diversity of scenes and incidents. The scenery is distinctly and characteristically American. In the liberal use of similes (I have counted fifty-one) he follows Homer and Vergil; Goethe has only one. They are short and extended, Biblical and profane, covering a wide range — which includes even Xerxes and his plane-tree. Some of them are truly exquisite.

The true story of Longfellow's source is familiar: the Reverend H. L. Conolly, a friend of Hawthorne's, had heard from a French Canadian the story of a young pair in Acadie, who, on the day of their intended marriage, had been separately transported to the English colonies. The bride spent the rest of her long life in searching for him, found him on his death-bed, and died from the shock. Mr. Conolly wished Hawthorne to use this tale for a romance, but he turned it over to Longfellow. This was freely acknowledged by the latter, who wrote to Hawthorne, after the publication of *Evangeline,* 'I thank you for resigning to me that legend of Acady. This success I owe entirely to you, for being willing to forego the pleasure of writing a prose tale which many people would have taken for poetry, that I might write a poem which many people take for prose.' The picture of the quiet Pennsylvania Hospital in Philadelphia had made a vivid impression on him as a youth of nineteen, and he re-

[115]

produced it in the final scene. He made a study of Canadian sources, introduced Indian and French folklore and local color (some of this derived from lively memories of rural France), owed something to Audubon and the admired Sealsfield for the cypress swamps and prairies of the south and west; even Banvard's *Panorama of the Mississippi* furnished him with realistic pictures. In writing to Freiligrath, he spoke of the 'descriptions of American scenery, to which I have endeavored to give the true and peculiar coloring of Nature.' Apart from all 'sources,' he recognized that 'the form and the poetry — they must come from my own brain.'

The metrical form of *Evangeline* proved a stone of stumbling and rock of offence to many of the poet's friends, who were upset by this 'hybrid measure.' It was a challenge to appreciate a new poetic mode. (That the mode was felt as 'new' was a damning comment on the prevalent reading of classic verse in academic institutions.) Motley, who actually held that Latin hexameters were characterized by 'recoil and springiness, like pulling out a piece of Indian rubber and letting it snap back again' [!!!], could not 'carry such English hexameters in his memory.'[1] Ten years later, Motley handsomely acknowledged his conversion to the opinion that these hexameters 'are as musical as is Apollo's lute.' The well-meaning apologies for Longfellow's metrics (explaining *difficilia per difficiliora*) are far harder to accept than the lines themselves. 'A trochee may take the place of a spondee' is simply darkening counsel by words: trochees are readily lengthened in English by pulling out the second syllable — whereby they *become* spondees. With this in mind, the poem conforms much more nearly to the ancient

[1] Posterity has reversed this verdict in the currency of such lines as, 'This is the forest primeval...'; 'Beautiful was the night...'; 'When she had passed, it seemed like the ceasing of exquisite music.'

[116]

musical pattern than the text of the *Æneid* in the 'snappy' scansion perpetrated in high schools.

Longfellow was thoroughly grounded in the ancient classical epics, which he read as measured verse, and for which he had an immediate appreciation. The liberties he allows are less frequent and distressing than those taken by Klopstock and Goethe. *Evangeline* contains one four-syllabled dactyl, which is no worse than Goethe's 'four-footed beast' in *Hermann und Dorothea*. The relatively high percentage of lines with five dactyls derives from Longfellow's instinctive consciousness that genuine dactyls can be more easily achieved in the Germanic languages than perfect spondees. Some of these flowing lines are very effective, such as the first verse of the poem, and

When the wild horses affrighted sweep by with the speed of the whirl-
wind.

Longfellow offers an unusual number of authentic spondees:

Out of the selfsame book, with the hymns of the church and the plain-
song; —
In-doors, warm by the wide-mouthed fireplace, idly the farmer; —
Many a farewell word and sweet good-night on the door-step; —
Like unto shipwrecked Paul on Melita's desolate sea-shore.

He has a distinct predilection for heavy spondees in the sixth foot: twelvemonth, smoke-wreaths, clock clicked, wolves howled, careworn, clothes-press — and a host of others. There are only four spondaic verses, a low average in comparison with Klopstock, or the first translation from Tegnér.[1]

The schooling in the use of this measure began with the first translation from Tegnér (who was influenced by Klopstock quite as much as by Goethe) in 1837. The later version of Tegnér's *Children of the Lord's Supper* (1841) showed a

---

[1] The relevancy of the Catullan distichs (cited in *Cambridge Edition*, 71), written after the publication of *Evangeline*, is far to seek.

marked increase in technical virtuosity. In retouching the short original poem, *To The Driving Cloud* (1845), Longfellow senses that it is formally superior to the translations from Tegnér — and Freiligrath, no mean judge in metrical matters, wrote to him, after having received this poem, that his hexameters were the best English ones he had ever read — the '*Driving Cloud* being even a progress compared to the *Children of the Lord's Supper.*' During the earliest stages of writing *Evangeline*, Longfellow was much taken by a translation from Homer in hexameters, appearing in Blackwood, and discussed it with Felton. 'This is the only way to translate Homer,' he declares in the diary; 'it gives at least some idea of him.' He recurs to the same subject later in the year: 'The English world is not yet awake to the beauty of that metre' — nor did his musical feeling lead him astray in this matter.

In 1848, Longfellow received a considerable importation of German books, including Börne's *Schriften* and Heine's *Atta Troll*. His keen interest in the German political poets of that stormy period is shown by an analysis of the portraits of ten of their number, contained in one of these volumes. He was much distressed by the reactionary suppression of the German Revolution. Still afflicted with neuralgia and defective eye-sight, he was faithfully aided by his gifted wife: the picture of their quiet evenings, devoted to the reading of literature, is most ingratiating. Thomas Buchanan Read recorded the scene:

> When she, fit bride for such as thou,
> (She with the calm and queenly brow),
> Read from the minstrel's page with tuneful voice and low.

They enjoyed together Jean Paul's *Levana* and *Campaner-Tal*, Schelling's essay on Dante ('like a dark cave with some gleaming stalactites hanging from the roof'), and Schefer's *Albrecht Dürer* ('an admirable art-novel'). At this time appeared Emmanuel Vitalis Scherb, a German poet from Basel, armed with a letter of introduction and an unfinished tragedy on the *Bauernkrieg*. 'He passed the afternoon with me, and we had much talk about the German poets.' (He was destined to pass many hours with the poet, for weal or woe.)

The New England novel, *Kavanagh*, appeared in 1849. Its author wrote it to his 'own satisfaction and delight,' and found it 'pleasant and easy work' — perhaps far too easy, though it gained enthusiastic praise from Emerson and Hawthorne. It contains dreary tracts of petty, undramatic preaching; a genial humorous spirit plays about it — and it seems to arrive nowhere. It is mentioned here merely because German critics find in its subjectivity, humor, and leaning toward idyllic *Kleinmalerei* a reflection of Jean Paul. Close upon this followed *The Seaside and the Fireside*, in which *The Building of the Ship* takes first place. The general structure at once suggests Schiller's *Bell*, which Longfellow knew and admired, and which he followed (like Peter) 'afar off.' A series of processes is accompanied by suggested comments and applications — but the subject-matter and treatment are wholly American. Keen-eyed foreign critics detect in the figure of the ship as bride of the sea a debt to Freiligrath's *Amphitrite* (1832), which contains these two lines:

> Der graue Meergott küsst
> Schäumend der Gattin Wangen.

They have *not* noted that both poems contain the word, 'Lascar.'

In the same volume, the poems *Twilight* and *The Fire of Drift-Wood* have a slight suggestion of Heine.

The following year, Longfellow read Goethe's *Campagne in Frankreich*, and 'finds it very interesting.' He sent a translation of Schelling's essay on Dante to Graham's Magazine, and ordered the formidable set of publications of the *Literaturverein* in Stuttgart. His lectures on Faust held up well, as is shown by the fact that a new college class wished to study that work. He assented, though he was convinced that it meant 'only one impediment more between me and the real work I have to do.' Before the summer vacation he had ended his lectures on the First Part of *Faust*, and gave a single concluding lecture on the Second Part, limiting his discourse to the First Scene and the Last Act. In the autumn term he repeated his introductory lecture on Faust to some law students, at their request.

The *Golden Legend* was faithfully wrought out during the years 1850 and 1851. Shortly before its completion, Longfellow confided to his diary that he had 'lost all enthusiasm about it,' and expected it to fail. It constituted, in fact, a new phenomenon in American letters, and enjoyed a great sale. The name (which has no essential connection with Jacobus de Voragine's *Legenda Sanctorum*) was chosen by the author 'because the story seems to me to surpass all other legends in beauty and significance.' That imperishable little epic, *Der arme Heinrich*, which furnishes the core of the story, and was written by the Swabian singer, Hartmann von Aue, about 1215, was accessible to Longfellow in Mailáth's *Altdeutsche Gedichte*, which he knew in Heidelberg, in 1836. His friend Rölker made for him a complete modern prose version of the Middle High German text.[1] Some of the most pretentious early critics were quite in the dark as to the source of the tale.[2] It was on November 27, 1839, that he

---

[1] The poet's copy of Mailáth, with significant marginal marks, is in Craigie House.
[2] See Münzer: *Die Quellen zu Longfellow's Golden Legend*, Dresden, 1898.

first recorded his interest in 'a drama on the old poetic legend
of *Der arme Heinrich*. The tale is exquisite. I have a heroine
as sweet as Imogen, could I but paint her so. [This 'heroine'
is not far to seek.] I think I must try this. But, first, a lecture on Jean Paul.'

This antedates by a full year that project which Longfellow
regarded as his chief life-work, 'a long and elaborate poem by
the holy name of Christ; the theme of which would be the
various aspects of Christendom in the Apostolic, Middle,
and Modern Ages' — a plan which was actually brought to
a close after more than thirty years of devoted labor, and
which good Father Baumgartner lauded as 'a bold confession
of faith, in the midst of a crooked, perverse, and gainsaying
generation.' It was only during the writing of this work that
the poet decided to use it as the Second Part of *Christus* —
and *The Golden Legend* may well be considered apart from
that enterprise.

The drama, which enormously transcends the simple epic
on which it is founded, and is about four times as long, is a
large panorama, exhibiting an encyclopedic grasp of human
history and culture; a symphony of many modes, covering
many phases of life; a *tour de force* in medievalism, having as
its chief model no less ambitious a pattern than Goethe's
Faust — which is not saying that it is a servile copy, or that
many other sources did not enter into its composition. The
resemblances are as obvious as they are numerous: here, if
anywhere, we may speak of 'borrowing.' The opening can-
tata form (which lent itself so well to Sullivan's and Liszt's
compositions) suggests various scenes in Goethe's work.
The first monologue, in Hans Sachs-meter, is plainly akin to
Faust's soliloquy, even in the metrical variations. Lucifer is
the (im)moral equivalent of Mephisto: his sudden appearance
in disguise; his hatred of sacred objects and symbols; his fear

that he may finally lose the soul of the Prince; his sneers at academic pedantry; his disguise as a priest, readily suggesting Mephisto's masquerade as professor — such details indicate that the American poet aimed to introduce these materials to his fellow-countrymen in their own tongue. Prince Henry, like Faust, is discovered sitting in a chamber in a tower at midnight; 'alone, ill, and restless.' The friar at work on the Gospel of John is akin to Faust at the same occupation; the name, 'Doctor Serafino,' at once brings to mind (with no other resemblance whatever) the 'Pater Seraphicus' in Goethe's last scene.

More specific resemblances to *Faust* abound: Prince Henry's long interview with Lucifer at the Vautsberg is obviously modeled upon the discussions between Faust and Mephisto in the Studierzimmer.

> The secret and the mystery
> Have baffled and eluded me,
> Unseen the grand result remains!

is almost a transcription from Faust's first monologue (lines 355 ff., Weimar Ed.). The joyful festivity of Easter, the revival of life and happiness which it brings

> .... and free from care
> The faces of the people shine

is a reflection of the scene, *Vor dem Tor* (808 ff.).

> What a gay pageant! what bright dresses!
> It looks like a flower-besprinkled meadow

is very close to

> Doch an Blumen fehlt's im Revier,
> Sie nimmt geputzte Menschen dafür (914 f.).

[122]

Prince Henry's swoon, after the 'draught of fire':

> Golden visions wave and hover,
> Golden vapors, waters streaming,
> Landscapes moving, changing, gleaming!

is a mere variant of the *Einschläferungs-Lied* (1447 ff.). The potion presented by Lucifer, with its workings, is quite akin to the draught in the *Hexenküche* (2519 ff.). The 'Black Paternoster' owes much to the same scene.

> They come, the shapes of joy and woe,
> The airy crowds of long ago,
> The dreams and fancies known of yore,
> That have been, and shall be no more

sounds like a direct translation from the *Zueignung*. Lucifer's advice:

> ... leave this labor
> Unto Time, the great Destroyer!

resembles *Faust*, 1365 ff.

The Scholar, in remarking:

> To tell the truth, I have arrived so lately,
> I hardly yet have had time to discern

is repeating the words of the *Schüler*:

> Ich bin allhier erst kurze Zeit (1868).

Lucifer's sneers at studies and old falsehoods, and his

> What a darksome and dismal place!

are in the spirit of

> Was ist das für ein Marterort? (1835 ff.).

The 'cobwebs' and 'dust' are related to *Faust*, 399 ff. and
6572 ff.

> Blighting all we breathe upon

is the equivalent of

> Das schmilzt und schrumpft vor eurem Hauch (11715).

The inquiries as to the disguised stranger at the drinking-
bout, as well as his impudent answers ('The Refectory')
evidently go back to the scene in Auerbach's Cellar.

Other parallels need no comment:

> ... this little flask
> Contains the wonderful quintessence
> The perfect flower and efflorescence
> Of all the knowledge man can ask!

> Ich grüsse dich, du einzige Phiole!...
> In dir verehr' ich Menschenwitz und Kunst.
> Du Inbegriff der holden Schlummersäfte (690 ff.).

> ... the undisturbed and deep
> Tranquility of endless sleep!...
> Headlong into the mysteries
> Of life and death I boldly leap

> Zu diesem Schritt sich heiter zu entschliessen,
> Und wär' es mit Gefahr, ins Nichts dahin zu fliessen (718 f.); —

The angel's 'Woe! woe!' and the 'Weh! weh!' of the
Geisterchor (1607).

> 'I have one thing to ask of you.' 'What is it?
> It is already granted.'

> 'Versprich mir, Heinrich!' 'Was ich kann!' (3414 f.).

> I have also a part in the play.

> Hab' ich doch meine Freude dran! (3543).

and the final words:

> He, too, is God's minister,
> And labors for some good
> By us not understood!
>
> Ein Teil von jener Kraft
> Die stets das Böse will und stets das Gute schafft (1335 f.).

It may be conceded that Longfellow fell short of creating an American *Faust*, but his gaze was fixed on no unworthy model.

The astounding medieval lore upon which Longfellow drew has been amply discussed in learned treatises; we are concerned with those in the German field. The vivid background of German life, and the wealth of folklore are too manifold to be fully accounted for. In 1848, Longfellow had acquired Scheible's *Kloster*, a rich quarry for older material. The Latin mottoes on the great bells are not taken directly from Schiller, as has been alleged; in the Bowdoin days, the young professor had noted from Sismondi's *Literature of the Dark Ages*, the Leonine verses:

> Laudo Deum verum, plebem voco, congrego clerum;
> Defunctos ploro, nimbum fugo, festaque honoro.

The rowdy sermon of Friar Cuthbert is not due to *Wallenstein*, but to the Dominican Father Barletta. The adventures of that medieval Rip van Winkle, Monk Felix, were taken directly from Mailáth's *Altdeutsche Gedichte*; the Fastrada-legend was found in Massmann, but may have been suggested by Wilhelm Müller's ballad, *Die Sage vom Frankenberger See*. The story of Christ and the Sultan's daughter is almost a direct translation from *Des Knaben Wunderhorn*, a beautiful copy of which was purchased in Heidelberg (1836). The Easter Play (including the comic touches) is in the authentic spirit of older German specimens, though the poet made much study of English Mysteries and Miracles, and the apocryphal gospels. The line, 'Still is the night,' sounds like an unconscious memory of Heine; the allusion to the Jews of Bacharach may also be derived from him — while the phrase, 'with lyre and sword' faintly suggests Körner, whose poems Longfellow owned and studied.

Freiligrath, while recognizing *The Golden Legend* as 'one of the finest leaves in your well-earned laurel-wreath,' felt that the 'old, homely, simple story of our *Armer Heinrich*' had been treated 'with too much *brilliancy*.' The thread of the original story was followed faithfully, in the main. 'Elsie's' didacticism in preaching to her parents is much toned down. At the beginning of the story, she is fifteen years old — more advanced in years than in the German original. Prince Heinrich is transported from his native Swabia to Hoheneck on the Rhine, a region with which Longfellow was more intimately acquainted. Hartmann's revolting *Aussatz* 'has no name,' or is 'a *kind* of leprosy,' — though the ceremony of living burial points to nothing less than this affliction itself. The constant element of *diablerie* owes nothing to Hartmann, but very much to Goethe. The suggestions, both to the Prince and the mother, come from this source; the operating physician (no unworthy figure in *Der arme Heinrich*) becomes Lucifer himself. The pious Hartmann ascribes the final healing to *der heilige Krist*, whereas Longfellow attributes it to 'a touch of St. Matthew's sacred bones.'

The poet's sympathetic penetration into the spirit of medieval religion has been praised by men of high authority: its yearning devotion, its spirit of complete renunciation. Longfellow's sensitive wife felt that it was 'almost too Catholic, and rather dangerous to publish in these excited times.' Certain vigorously painted scenes (*At Sea*; *The School of Salerno*) bear comparison with Browning's liveliest pictures. The chief characters, as in the case of Tennyson's *Idyls of the King*, are sentimentalized to conform to Victorian taste: it would be difficult to picture Hartmann's hero as discoursing on 'Æolian strings,' or referring to the 'Hesperides.' The priceless humor of the monks of Hirschau and of the Miracle Play goes far toward offsetting this tendency. Longfellow's unwavering devotion to 'the common man,' which his favored social position never corrupted, may also be detected in this work. The galloping rhythm of *The Road to Hirschau* stands by itself in the realm of metrics.

Certain anachronisms are neither more numerous nor disturbing than those to be found in most great poetry. *Little Red Ridinghood* was hardly a current tale in Germany in the early thirteenth century; Erwin von Steinbach flourished about 1318; Saint John Nepomuck came to his death in 1393 — while Barletta, who furnished Friar Cuthbert's sermon, lived in the fifteenth century.

After *The Golden Legend*, Longfellow uttered no volume before *Hiawatha*, in November, 1855. This interval he described as the 'most unproductive period of my life.' He wrote down only a few poems: 'All faculty of song seems to have gone out of me.' Severe neuralgia added its burden, and the work of teaching was exceedingly heavy: on one day, 'six hours in the lecture-room.' *Faust* held the center of his interest; he was 'always afraid of leaving the most important thing unsaid.' In December, 1853, he admitted three unknown damsels from Boston who begged this concession, to his *Faust* lectures, stationing them 'on the front seat. It was a little awkward, but passed off without trouble.' They continued to appear, until he finished the First Part. His private reading of German was not suspended. *Wilhelm Meister* was re-read with vivid interest. The chapter in which Meister is *désillusionné* in regard to Marianne he found 'very

[127]

powerful.' Of the whole work, he said: 'What a gallery of portraits! what variety! what richness of coloring, — and what a collection of tainted ducks! If this be, as I suppose it is, a picture of German society at the close of the last century, it was the most promiscuous thing imaginable.'

The 'Germanians' of Boston invited him to become a Director of their concerts; on December 3, 1853, he attended one of these, which presented Wagner's music: 'strange, original, and somewhat barbaric.'

solicitude for the needy, sustained work on the translation of
Dante, the preparation of a number of volumes of verse, and
the change of scene afforded by travel — all these combined
to lighten the pain of a wound that never healed. But
throughout the long remaining years there were ever-recur-
rent pangs of poignant memory. These sacred recollections
found no direct expression in published verse, though they
vibrate, in subdued undertones, through the later poetry:

> [He] knew the life-long martyrdom,
> The weariness, the endless pain
> Of waiting for some one to come
> Who nevermore would come again.

The fourth, and final, sojourn in Europe was undertaken
in May, 1868, and lasted for fifteen months. For this trip,
Longfellow assembled a family group of some ten persons,
and the expedition resembled a *Völkerwanderung* rather than
an *iter scholasticum*. Italy and England were the favored
scenes, and German territory was traversed cursorily. So
many distinguished honors were tendered that the recipients
were well-nigh 'killed by kindness.' The 'busy idleness'
involved in leading such an invasion precluded any sustained
studies; diary and correspondence had to be slighted, and it
is quite obvious that no literary harvest could be gathered
during this crowded recreational outing.

Our concluding task is to survey the poet's relation to
Germany during the remaining years. The correspondence
with Freiligrath was continued, and there were many traveling Germans who called at Craigie House to pay their
respects. After Rölker had brought an account of a typical
bourgeois wedding in Cambridgeport, Longfellow exclaimed
in his diary: 'The Germans have so much poetry in their
natures, and in their lives!' On one occasion, he went to the
Police Court and 'got off' some poor German women un-

justly accused of stealing apples. On the tenth of November, 1859, he took part in the celebration of the hundredth anniversary of Schiller's birth. This affair, which he described as 'the great event of the week,' was held in the Boston Music Hall, and offered much music, as well as speeches in German and English. Probably during this period he translated for Sumner, in the original form, the eight elegiac verses of Schiller's *Columbus* (unpublished) — doubtless with reference to Sumner's heroic political action in the face of opposition. Quite late in life, he walked to The Riverside Press to enlist interest in the publication of Mr. Kroeger's *Specimens of the Minnesingers*. Four years before his death, he received an elaborate invitation, written by William Cullen Bryant, to appear at the Goethe Club in New York City: 'You will certainly nowhere meet with those who more delight in what you have written, or who would receive greater pleasure from your visit.'

Intimate and pertinent allusions to German matters (sometimes quite veiled) cropped out so frequently as to show that the hidden springs still flowed freely. In writing to a lady on the subject of housekeeping, he pointed his sermon by adding:

> Then I think of Schiller's beautiful description of the wife in his 'Song of the Bell,' and how the German women beautify and dignify their household cares, and how the American women do not, — which is a great pity and a great mistake: for life is very much what we make it, and if we call duty by the name of drudgery we degrade it.

In 1871, he discussed *Faust* with Agassiz, who made a pencil sketch giving his own idea of the significance of the pentagram (l. 1396): a flat projection of the buds of growth in many plants gives five equidistant points, which, being alternately connected by lines, make a perfect pentagram.

Drawn by Agassiz to explain
the Pentagraph Jan. 17. 1871

SKETCH MADE BY AGASSIZ TO ILLUSTRATE PENTAGRAM IN 'FAUST'
Inscription by Longfellow

Longfellow, who, like Browning, was inclined to make poetic capital of almost any curious bit of information,[1] gave an elaborated exposition of this theory in *The Divine Tragedy* ('Second Passover,' scene XI: 'Simon Magus and Helen of Tyre').

When Longfellow wrote to a young lady that 'poetry is the flower and perfume of thought... "clothing the common-place of life with golden exhalations of the dawn," ' he was quoting directly from *Wallensteins Tod*, V, III. In reading the *Frogs* of Aristophanes, he was struck by the thought that it was a good introduction for the Second Part of *Faust*. In 1881, a lady caller immediately suggested to his mind the Baroness in *Wilhelm Meister*.

Rauch's statuette of Goethe, which Longfellow bought at Heidelberg in 1836, continued to stand on his writing-desk; it is still there. Mr. J. T. Fields was impressed, in 1871, by the likeness of Longfellow's private rooms to those of a German student or professor — 'a Goethean aspect of simplicity and space everywhere.' Reading for his own satisfaction, and commenting without an aim at publicity, he compassed much of the German classics and contemporary writings, discussing Goethe's letters with Rölker, and re-reading *Wilhelm Meister* (at Nahant); of Lewes's *Life of Goethe* he said: 'a very clever and judicious book. The best we have had as yet, giving the great German as he really was.' He read Eckermann's *Gespräche mit Goethe*, and an English translation of *Hermann und Dorothea*; likewise, the *Tag- und Jahres-Hefte*, and Schiller's *Briefwechsel mit Körner*:

> Taken together, they give a very different view of Goethe from the one usually given, and show a man not holding himself apart from others, but longing for sympathy, and very lenient

[1] A notable example was his felicitous, though far-fetched, use of the 'Lapland Song' in *My Lost Youth*.

in his judgments. Schiller and Körner do not spare his weaknesses. Extracts from these and similar works would make the best life of Goethe.

Reading *Don Carlos*, he compared it with Alfieri's *Filippo*:

> More poetical, but not so simply tragic. Alfieri's tragedy is the drop of deadly poison in a ring; Schiller's is the same, diluted and drunk from a silver-chased goblet. Schiller's is a very noble poem, affluent in thought and diction, but too long and too intricate for a tragedy.

Voss's *Briefe*, Lessing's *Emilia Galotti*, Schlegel's lectures on the German Drama, Grillparzer's *Ahnfrau* ('extremely effective'), and Heine's *Lutetia* are among the books read for personal edification. The last, with the comment: 'spicy descriptions of Paris and Parisian notabilities in the days of Louis Philippe.' Grimm's *Michael Angelo*, by no means his only source, was faithfully studied for his own drama of like name: 'a most interesting and charmingly written book.'

He accompanied Mrs. Fields, of Boston, to hear Wilhelm Jordan recite his *Nibelungenlied*. The lady records:

> The reader twisted his face up into frightful knots, and delivered his poem with vast apparent satisfaction to himself, if not to his audience... It was in the old sentimental German style familiar to the readers of that literature. Longfellow amused me as we walked home by imitating the sing-song voice we had been following all the evening. He also recited in the original that beautiful little poem by Platen, *In der Nacht, in der Nacht*, in a most delightful manner. 'Ah!' he said, 'to translate a poem properly it must be done into the metre of the original.'

The output of direct translations from the German was very small: in 1870, while preparing a supplement to the *Poets and Poetry of Europe*, he made the charming versions of Goethe's *Wanderer's Night-Songs* which stand at the head of all similar attempts.[1] For the same work he translated Platen's *Mut und Unmut* ('Remorse'), which almost captures the haunting music of the original.[2] The interlude, *Martin Luther* (1871), contains a somewhat turgid rendering of *Ein' feste Burg*, which cannot be termed the happiest among such efforts. In 1879 was published the translation of *Forsaken*, the first stanza of which had been used as the heading for Book II of *Hyperion*. Mahlmann's *Allah* (Thirza's song in the tale, *Benno*) seems to belong to this period: Longfellow's version has enjoyed much esteem, to which Chadwick's song-setting has doubtless contributed.

Finally, a glance at Longfellow's own later works which show traces of German influence. Part Second of the *Tales of a Wayside Inn* (1872) includes 'The Cobbler of Hagenau,' a tale with a German background, built on the story of Tetzel and his indulgences (from d'Aubigné's *Histoire de la Réformation*), and containing allusions to *Reineke Fuchs*, the Meistersinger, Brant and Eulenspiegel. The third group of the *Tales* (1873) gives a grim picture of Charlemagne as the 'man of iron,' and contains the *very* Boccaccian tale of his daughter, in *Emma and Eginhard*. Both of these stories are taken from Latin sources. *Elizabeth* (a milder *Miles Standish*) is the last poem in hexameter, 'pale and quiet,' as its author remarks, but containing the ever-memorable 'Ships that pass in the night.' In the following interlude, this story is spoken of as

> ... worthy of some German bard,
> Hebel, or Voss, or Eberhard,
> Who love of humble themes to sing,
> In humble verse.

[1] *Ueber allen Gipfeln* shows a great advance from the translation in *Hyperion*.
[2] J. T. Fields speaks of *two* 'translations from Platen's *Night-Songs*' at this time. He perhaps confused *Remorse* with the lyrics from Goethe.

In the third *Birds of Passage* (1873), the poem *Vox Populi* is perhaps suggestive of Heine's manner; *The Brook and the Wave,* assuredly.

The collection, *Poems of Places,* was undertaken in 1874 — the last of the thirty-one volumes appearing in 1879. Naturally it recalled vividly 'the bright days when I was young' —

> And towers of old cathedrals tall,
> And castles by the Rhine.

The editor added no new poems of his own relating to Germany.

The *Hanging of the Crane* (for which the author received three thousand dollars — *not* at his own solicitation) consists, as does Schiller's *Bell,* of uniform introductory stanzas, each followed by illustrative scenes. It must be admitted that this work did not evoke general rapture on the part of the public. *Morituri Salutamus* (1875) cites, among examples of productive old age:

> Goethe at Weimar, toiling to the last,
> Completed Faust when eighty years were past.

The *Masque of Pandora,* derived chiefly from the Greek tragedy, has suggestions of the Second Part of *Faust,* especially in the chorus of Oreades, Waters, Winds, and Forests. Goethe's *Prometheus* was not drawn upon. The Chorus of the Eumenides suggests Goethe's *Iphigenie.*

Kéramos (1878), again, is built on the general plan of Schiller's *Bell;* its longer passages, however, have to do only with visions of various remote regions concerned with the production of pottery. The tribute to *Bayard Taylor* (1878) compares his books with the statues standing about the tomb of Maximilian I., at Innsbruck.

Ultima Thule (1880), Longfellow's last volume, is a final

assertion of his unwavering allegiance to his high poetic mission, as is nobly expressed in its Horatian motto:

> ... Precor, integra
> Cum mente, nec turpem senectam
> Degere, nec cithara carentem.

The breezy humor and dialogue-form of the second 'Folk-Song' relate it to German types. *Mad River* (1882), in form and metrical movement, shows a resemblance to Goethe's *Der Junggesell und der Mühlbach*. The posthumous fragment, *The Children's Crusade*, has some lines which remind one of Heine's *Wallfahrt nach Kevlaar*:

> In Cologne the bells were ringing,
> In Cologne the nuns were singing...
> While above the band devoted
> Consecrated banners floated.

The elegiac distichs, written for the most part in 1881, closely resemble in form and spirit those of Goethe and Schiller — though they borrow very little of their content from that source.

The last stanza which Longfellow wrote, about one week before his death, was a declaration of independence from older traditions, a summons to advance into a new era:

> O Bells of San Blas, in vain
> Ye call back the Past again!
> The Past is deaf to your prayer;
> Out of the shadows of night
> The world rolls into light;
> It is daybreak everywhere.

CHAPTER X

A Summary

THE status of Germans in the United States during the first half of the nineteenth century cannot be termed imposing: possibly something of the odium deriving from the Hessian mercenaries of the Revolution still lingered in popular consciousness — though there was nothing like a systematic boycott against Germans, as such. One of the most honored early immigrants was Dr. Charles Follen, whose liberal political principles forced him to seek refuge in America in 1824; he was accompanied by Carl Beck, who became celebrated as one of Harvard's most distinguished professors. Follen was advised by Lafayette to find a home in Cambridge, because of the liberal views of President Kirkland (1810–1829), and the presence there of Everett and Ticknor, both of whom had studied in Göttingen. Through the efforts of solicitous friends, a fund was raised by private subscription, which made it possible to secure his appointment for five years (1830–1835) as first Professor of the German Language and Literature in Harvard College. When these funds were exhausted, the college was unable to continue the engagement, and the professorship lapsed. Follen, who shone in literature, philosophy, theology, and gymnastics, became a most respected citizen (he married a Cabot!); he recorded, during the time of his professorship, 'my attachment to this glorious country grows daily.' Writing to Germany from Cambridge, he gave the following opinion as to certain elements of the populace:

> The mass of the people are here far better instructed than in any part of Europe with which I am acquainted. Our German

emigrants, who settle in Pennsylvania, with the Irish (who commonly find employment on the high roads and canals, and as servants), are most uncivilized, but are, nevertheless, highly esteemed; the first, as industrious cultivators of the soil; the last, as day-laborers and servants. Many of them, that is, of the Germans (for the Irish soon get rid of their earnings), rise by their industry to the station of respectable citizens, and most of them are prosperous, and frugal, though hospitable. But they have not the smallest inclination to give their children a better education, and are even strengthened in this by their clergy, generally ignorant fanatics (with many honorable exceptions), who are inclined to put down every attempt to open their minds, lest thus heresy should be introduced. This is the state of things in the German villages. The German mechanics and traders who came here succeed tolerably well, for the most part, but they spoil everything with the inhabitants, because they foolishly criticize every thing in this country, and pretend that they have been great gentlemen at home; so that I often have occasion to wonder at the good-nature of the people, who do not fail, notwithstanding their rudeness, to acknowledge and respect the good qualities of those who blame and ridicule them, at the same time that they find among them liberty and support....

In learned men and literary institutions, the Americans are far behind the Germans, though the progress of the people since their independence (a period of fifty years) is inconceivably great.

The influence of men like Ticknor (world-known as the historian of Spanish Literature), Everett, Bancroft, Cogswell, Motley, and Francis Lieber did much to add to the prestige of Germany among highly cultivated people, though the general population was influenced slowly. It is symptomatic that Longfellow's father wrote his son, in 1827, 'there is no gentleman in this state [Maine] who is master of the German language.' It was Ticknor who brought about Longfellow's studious adventure in Göttingen, from which we date the poet's firm bonds with Germany. It would be an exaggeration to assert that Germany 'made' our American poet: a host of other, and more important, factors united in this process. The eight months in Spain were especially potent in fixing a romantic love for the warmth and color of the South: the youth was so 'homesick for Spain' that he was almost loath to move on to his year in Italy. These impressions never wore out. As late as 1877, having never revisited the country, he wrote that vivid reminiscent poem, *Castles in Spain*:

> How much of my young heart, O Spain,
> Went out to thee in days of yore!

Bürger, Goethe, Heine and Richter seem to have been the first German authors who engaged his more intimate interest. Goethe, who penetrated his whole life and grew constantly in his esteem, undoubtedly helped him to turn, from a merely idyllic and romantic contemplation of life, to sterner issues. *Faust* always subtended a wide arc of Longfellow's horizon: in *The Golden Legend* he too ambitiously strove to create a work which might stand at its side — and for this he thought it no robbery to 'take over' many features of Goethe's work, but they are far from constituting all the sources of that spiritual drama.

Richter, especially after the Heidelberg residence, held an important and perhaps disproportionate place, and bulked largely in Longfellow's lectures on German literature.. The sequence, Sterne-Richter-Heine, is not easy to disentangle, but it is evident that Longfellow's youthful prose style was largely colored (most notably in *Hyperion*) by 'the Only One.' Literal borrowings can hardly be proved. Matthisson early attracted our poet's sympathetic attention, and must be reckoned (along with 'Hebel, or Voss, or Eberhard') among those 'German bards' who encouraged him 'to sing of humble themes in humble verse.' Like Goethe, Uhland and Heine, he derived much from the German *Volkslied*. Schiller's *Bell* furnished the architectural structure for three longer poems. Various more sporadic literary influences are treated of in the body of this work. When certain poems are effectively marshaled, they make a fair sum, but it must be adduced that Longfellow *did* write some other things. Undoubtedly, a sentimental response to impressions from the external world, and a mystical interpretation of these values derive from the Teutonic atmosphere: 'I leave the gayeties of Paris for the dreams of Germany,' is an unpublished note in the diary of May 26, 1842. His absorption in German prose and poetry at Heidelberg doubtless shows itself in the greater richness, spontaneity and vigor of the poems written after those days. Nor should one omit his training in scholarly habits and methods, or his extensive study of German sources in his exploration of subject-matter for his verse.

Longfellow's affection for the Germans was genuine and lasting. He admired their heartiness, their love of art; the color, music and song which made poetry of their daily lives; their genius for productive work, their sincere craftsmanship, their intellectual honesty. After his arrival at Göttingen, in 1829, he wrote to his father that he 'liked Göttingen more and more daily.' 'I do indeed love the Germans,' he confessed in *Hyperion*; 'the men are so hale and hearty, and the Fräuleins so tender and true!' Reading *Reynke de Vos* in Holland (1835), he praised the old German poets: 'they sing in sunshine among leaves and flowers.' In 1849, his memory goes back: 'A mild winter morning, like Germany — the south of Germany, — the region of the middle Rhine.' The poem *Nuremberg* is a heartfelt tribute to some of the most admirable and permanent traits of German character.

Something over three months' systematic study in Dresden and Göttingen, reinforced by constant private work at Bowdoin, had given Longfellow a fair practical command of the language by the time he left America for his intensive training in German, on April 10, 1835. Turning to Scandinavian territory and studies, he found this medium fully adequate for learned contacts in those parts. While his stay in the northern countries was not long, it was significant in laying a solid philological and historical foundation for later studies. His almost incredible industry in Heidelberg, supplemented by the valuable associations of Marienberg (1842), gave him a complete practical virtuosity in the use of the language. This achievement had been gained in the face of his revered mother's advice: 'I do not believe the language, that is, the pronunciation of it, would ever be of much advantage to you.' The living tongue, with its crisp idioms, became a second nature: he caught its exact spirit; he dropped into it unconsciously in conversation and correspondence.

On the whole, it is quite possible that Germany owes as much to Longfellow as Longfellow to Germany: in the early days of his teaching, there was no center where so ample a survey of its literature was offered, as at Harvard. The work was undertaken in the spirit of the great European universities, and the ideal on which it was centered was that of mastery of the field by the man who presented it. The young professor had many other subjects to teach, but (with the possible exception of Dante) there was none which rivalled German literature in his interest. He made it his duty to refresh and deepen his knowledge by continual reading and study. His private library grew, and he built up that of the college. In the choice of subject-matter, he was a pioneer, and followed no beaten track. The eighteen years of his academic teaching accomplished much toward the breaking-down of narrow Anglo-Saxon prejudice. Goethe, Heine, Richter, Hoffmann, and Uhland claimed a large share of his interest, with an ever-increasing emphasis of Goethe. High praise has been accorded him for his special gift in reviving the middle ages.

Breaking with dry academic pedantry, he gave sprightly verdicts that were of first-hand independence. His lively presentation was in accord with sound pedagogic method. In approaching alien values, he used (as he expressed it) 'strong, simple, healthy common-sense.' There was a straightforward reality in going directly at the heart of the subject, without excursions from the first intent of the author. That 'vague and fanciful philosophy,' (parodied in 'Glimpses into Cloud Land' in *Hyperion*), which leads directly into the mists of Νεφελοκοκκυγία, and which constitutes the Great White Plague of much German scholarship, never intrigued him: he humorously tempered its over-sentimentality, cloudiness and discursiveness.

His direct translations of German poems, faultless in form and spirit, did much to win the interest of a people not too highly endowed with a love of song. *Hyperion*, which enjoyed a very large circulation, offered a broad and new picture of German life and literature. The *Poets and Poetry of Europe*, *Poems of Places*, and *Poetic Aphorisms* brought alien subjects into the popular consciousness. Something might be added as to Longfellow's promotion of German music, of which he was an intelligent and enthusiastic lover. By correspondence and personal contacts with significant Germans, he strengthened the ties of friendship between the two countries, and evoked a new respect and love for America.

Some discussion of the currency of Longfellow's works in German translation would seem to be in place — but the very complete catalogue published by Paul Morin makes

[143]

this superfluous.[1] Not only the lyrics, but the longer works in prose and verse have been repeatedly presented to German readers in their own tongue: Freiligrath's *Hiawatha; The Golden Legend*, in the version of the Baroness von Hohenhausen; Karl Knortz's *Evangeline* and *Miles Standish* may be mentioned particularly.

[1] *Les Sources de l'Œuvre de H. W. L.*, Paris 1913. An imposing, though less complete, list is to be found also in the Appendix to S. Longfellow's *Life*.

CHAPTER XI

Concerning Longfellow

AN ODD theory prevails, in certain quarters, that Longfellow's life moved upon an easy, beaten track, along the line of least resistance. This cannot be squared with the fact that, from his boyhood days, he was firmly convinced as to his calling to play a part in American letters, and that he devoted himself to this mission with unfailing zeal and unremitting hard work. The tenacity with which he, a boy of nineteen, fought through his purpose to study in Germany — against the 'set' opposition of his influential parents, whose substantial sacrifices had made his European sojourn possible; the courage with which he projected (three years later) the entire reform of American higher education, and professed himself ready to tackle the job, single-handed; the sturdy independence shown in refusing the lowering of rank proposed by Bowdoin College — such manifestations argue a rugged purpose which triumphed over difficult obstacles.

The soil from which his harvest was to grow was cultivated with unwavering steadfastness of purpose; the maturity of his mind ensured a 'severe, chaste, lofty-thoughted style of poetry,' worthy of Apollo; a sensitiveness to the more delicate values of existence. 'Your fine organization and poetical genius make you a sort of Italy among human beings,' wrote Hillard, and the world responded readily to the vibrant instrument of his nature. What he had resolved in youth, he pursued to the end of life. How resolutely he strove for full knowledge, how amply he 'drew from deep cisterns,' is plain to anyone who follows his career. He must be accounted a notable American 'humanist,' in the strict meaning of that abused word.

The scope of this book does not allow for an extended survey of his mastery of the ancient classics, in which he was thoroughly grounded, and from which he drew nourishment, refreshment, and clarity; simplicity, serenity, and sureness of touch. As undergraduate at Bowdoin, he made so brilliant a rendering of one of the odes of Horace, that one of the trustees, who was present as 'Examiner,' never forgot it, and was later influenced by it to present the name of the young graduate in candidacy for the proposed Professorship of Modern Languages. Horace remained a favorite, and furnished the significant motto for his last volume of poems.[1] In 1872, we have an ingratiating view of the poet reading Horace daily with his young daughter. He was on familiar terms with Lucretius, Plautus, Vergil, Ovid, Catullus; Homer, the Greek tragedians and lyric poets, even the Church Fathers were included in his chosen private reading. Such a sweep of horizon freed him from provincial pedantry and self-complacency; he deplored the fact that 'the typical Bostonian speaks as if he were the Pope'; he so consistently avoided the parade of learning that superficial critics are inclined to belittle his acquisitions. 'All Prefaces and the like are like labels coming out of the mouths of people in some poor pictures.'

Serenity and harmony are chief notes of Longfellow's temperament:

> Be not like a stream that brawls
> Loud with shallow waterfalls,
> But in quiet self-control
> Link together soul and soul.

[1] See J. P. Pritchard: *The Horatian Influence upon Longfellow. American Literature*, IV, 22. The 'influence' is the general one of Horace's ideas.

He did not flare out in convulsive eruptions, but moved, like Goethe, *ohne Hast, aber ohne Rast.* His sensitive instinct was for restraint, for tenderness: for quiet effects, for 'sweet, sunny Southern words.' 'It is with thoughts as with money,' he wrote in 1826: 'those who have most appear before the world in a plain dress.'

Neurotic younger writers find these tendencies difficult to condone, but, as Mr. Herbert Gorman so admirably reminds them, in his preface to Thornton Wilder's *Cabala*: 'such things as suavity, discipline, and classicism still exist.' His eye was never fixed on popularity: 'The talent of success is nothing more than doing well whatever you do — without a thought of fame.' 'The poet must keep true to his calling, and bide his time' (*Hyperion*). Longfellow was not a Byron, a Poe, a Hawthorne, or a Whitman — but Hawthorne's devoted and admiring friendship is symptomatic of a kinship of soul; even Poe paid his unqualified homage to *The Hymn to the Night, The Beleaguered City*, and *The Skeleton in Armor.* He lived in an environment for the most part removed from desperate struggles and furious passions; he was reared in a period which a recent biographer of Byron terms 'the damnable epoch of triumphant tameness' — in Longfellow's case, as 'tame' as the air and the sunshine.

Worse than all, Longfellow wrote the *Psalm of Life*, with all its platitudes! Such 'platitudes' were not distasteful to the Greeks, or Milton, or Schiller, or Goethe ('*Edel sei der Mensch!*'), or Wordsworth; they have fortified many drooping souls. The *Golden Milestone* is quite in the spirit of Horace, who abounds in such platitudes as are involved in putting into succinct and cogent form the crystallized experiences of the race.

The pathos and tragedy of life had their reflection in his

[147]

sensitive nature (Heaven knows, he was to drink deeply of those bitter waters!). Returning to his early home, in 1837, he confided to his notebook that, in his own soul, 'in the gradual alternation of years, dark, serious melancholy thoughts were springing up to take the place of the glad, green vision of his boyhood.' But, along with extreme sensitiveness, he had an essential robustness, which expressed itself with spontaneous abandon: the spirit and dash of *The Leap of Roushan Beg*; the stalwart humor in *The Golden Legend*; the full-blooded *Northern Sagas* and *King Witlaf's Drinking-Horn*; the Boccaccian *Emma and Eginhard* were the work of a man who knew other sides of life than the fireside. And he was anointed with a full drop of the priceless and saving grace of humor. Even to question this obvious fact, would argue a mind superior to mere accuracy. He was a member of a brilliant circle, which flashed wit; his own was always emergent and pertinent. Of a certain general, who had unsuccessfully tried to involve the United States in a war with England, he wrote: 'He has on his own private account declared a war against the English grammar, which he carries on vigorously, and successfully.' Of a pretentious young poet, who 'patronized' the trees at Craigie House, he said: 'It was as if he gave a certificate to all the neighboring vegetation.' He mentioned a lady who wore flowers 'on the congregation-side of her bonnet.' Of Caleb Cushing's dinner speech: 'It contained all Lemprière's Classical Dictionary and part of Adams's Latin Grammar.' 'Life, like French poetry, is imperfect without the feminine rhyme'; 'Beethoven's music, like the Latin verbs *odi* and *memini*, though past in form has always a present signification'; 'the house leaks like a friend to whom you have confided an important secret'; 'you might think me growing old, — which would be a great mistake: I have done that already'; 'if I were Briareus, or a disembodied echo, I could not answer the multitude of letters.'

In that early Confession of Faith, *Hyperion*, he showed sound sense in stabbing the vagaries of authors who 'keep themselves aloof from the world, apart from our fellow-men.... The poet should live in the world, in contact with other minds.' He chose (and this is a chief claim to his title of 'American' poet) native, near-at-hand, realistic subjects — symbolically indicated by *Gaspar Becerra*, who substituted indigenous oak for 'precious wood from a distant Easterly island'; also in the sonnet, *The Descent of the Muses.* This quality is the secret of his success in bringing poetry into the lives of multitudes of the common people.

In the face of conventions which strutted as Fundamental Laws, and whose rigor we can hardly estimate nowadays,[1] he was a bold innovator, who repeatedly showed the pioneer spirit in breaking with established traditions. 'American' he assuredly was, and nothing could be more futile than the attempt to classify him among those who are passive reflectors of European influence. He sought culture from European sources, and defended this sort of cosmopolitanism in *Kavanagh*, where he praised the tenderness of the Germans, the passion of the Spaniards, the vivacity of the French, and the solid sense of the English — but this argues no tame subserviency. Before he had come back from his first full years on the continent, an influential cosmopolitan friend [2] wrote from Boston: 'Your devotion to New England is delightful! I was very sure Europe would not spoil *you.*' When in Rome, at the very height of his European celebrity, Longfellow put down the *ritornella*:

[1] A literary friend objected to that rugged and grandiose poem, *The Lighthouse*, because it was not sufficiently 'regular.'

[2] MS letter from M. C. Derby, April 6, 1829. In Craigie House.

[149]

Se il Papa mi donasse Campidoglio
E mi dicesse, 'lascia andar sta figlia' (*America*)
Quella che amava prima, quella voglio.

He refused an Italian decoration, 'as an American citizen, a Protestant, and Republican.' England he called 'a beloved mother country, for which I have strong affection,' but there were times when he was constrained to cry out: 'The truth is, I never desire to see an Englishman, or any foreigner more than once. They grow inexpressibly tiresome with their crude opinions about the country. I have rarely met one who desired information. On the contrary, they desire to give you *their* opinion.'

Intense patriotism was the chief bond between himself and his closest friend, Sumner, though he was always averse from politics as a subject of social discourse. Loyalty to the Union, and the high sacrifices of war did not lead him to refuse to write one hundred autographs for the Chattanooga Fair in aid of Southern sufferers.

We have reached the point where we must face the heinous charge of Respectability, which at present threatens to overcast the fame of our poet. The heroic Puritan ideal contemplated the actual establishment of the Kingdom of God on earth — human nature to the contrary, notwithstanding. New England, during the first half of the nineteenth century, was one of the places where the assertion of theoretical Christian ethics most nearly squared with practices: it may be conceded that there were developed admirable types of temperate, wholesome, highly refined people, who grew up during the trying of this 'noble experiment' — which has some claim to be considered America's most interesting contribution to social experience. Henrietta Dana Skinner, who was brought up in the very heart of this society, and who cast herself, in due time, into the motherly arms of the

[150]

Catholic Church, makes, in *An Echo from Parnassus*, a gallant protest against the dark picture which is painted of the gloom and severity of Massachusetts life at the time. The stiff and dour personages whom the twentieth century has conjured up did not exist: 'they are figures of straw, which, as I can testify vigorously, bear little or no resemblance to the living figures of my youthful memories.' There was nothing 'mask-like' in the faces of Longfellow or his friends; the women of this environment were typical females of pure English ancestry, but they had not horse faces, buck teeth and big feet — nor were their manners defensively sharp and assertive.

In more recent years, Americans have been shamed out of their respect for the New England Tradition by alien influences, the final outcome of which is not easy to forecast: *Wohin mit dem Freud?* These things are not altogether new discoveries, for Longfellow, himself, in 1842, made mildly ironic reference to 'young ladies and young men in America who maintain that "nature must not be interfered with in any way."' Mr. Thornton Wilder considers it a 'European' thesis, 'Never try to do anything against the bent of human nature.' The same human nature, 'pawing to get free its hinder parts,' demands a faun-like abandonment, illustrated by South Sea islanders, Hollywood divorcés, and other lesser breeds without the Law, who 'have never heard that love can be a sin.' The word 'love' involves a certain ambiguity: its definition by a Longfellow and a Gautier cannot be brought under one hat. For the former, it meant constant and growing security and happiness; for the latter, a restless dread of staleness and failing desire. *La satiété vient en mangeant. Sir Christopher* (in the 'Wayside Inn') is a rollicking, delectable satire on militant anti-Puritan ethics.

Longfellow was not an orthodox Christian, but he honorably accepted abstinence as a social demand: he was actually attracted by the ideal of unique loyalty and devotion; he held that elemental 'human nature' has no rights which social evolution is bound to respect. Great ideas are mightier than passions. To his early Göttingen notebook (1829) he confided his contempt of one who was 'beating to arms against humanity, and expecting the walls of virtue and common-sense to fall down at the blast of his ram's horn.' His whole thesis is stated in the lines from *Manrique*:

> A life of honor and of worth
> .... far exceeds
> That base and sensual life, which leads
> To want and shame.

Woman was sublimated to a divinity. 'You were ever,' wrote one of the young lady friends of his college days, 'an admirer of the sex; but they seemed to you something enshrined and holy — to be gazed at and talked with, and nothing further.' While residing in Göttingen (1829), he wrote (during an excursion to Holland): 'What a homily of the pure heart and innocent affections did I read in the sweet countenances around me.' He rather annoyed Miss Crowninshield, on the second European trip (1835), by asserting: 'A wife should know nothing of such physical concerns. I would rather live on bread and water than eat the nicest dinner in the world if my wife had been obliged to cook it for me.' Having heard a lecture on 'Womanhood': 'I do not like to have woman discussed in public. Something within me rebels at the profanation.'

This principle envelops with blamelessness his long, unchaperoned tours with young ladies. And when, *moriturus*, he speaks his last words to his aged classmates, he has this to say of the Bowdoin professors:

Whose simple lives, complete and without flaw,
Were part and parcel of great Nature's law.

The stream of natural feelings never burst its banks — a situation which was so highly irritating to young Werther, as it has proved to later *Stürmer und Dränger*.

The present writer does not assert, at this time, that these inhibitions constitute a universal mandate — but we may possibly be permitted to study their effects in one life-case. Because thou hast cakes and ale, shall there be *no* virtue? Domestic ties, if attainable, knit ever more firmly by increasing devotion, offer many obvious advantages as contrasted with more hectic delights:

Haile wedded Love, mysterious Law, true source
Of human ofspring, sole proprietie
In Paradise of all things common else.

It worked. Measured by the joy-of-living, Longfellow may be reckoned one of the happiest of mortals. It is not over-seemly to peer into domestic relations, but the complete fulfillment of an unsuppressed affection is a matter which concerns every pilgrim through this Vale of Tears. Longfellow's programme was laid down, theoretically and prophetically, in *Hyperion*:

He is the Happy Man, who blessed with modest ease, a wife and children, sits enthroned in the hearts of his family, and knows no other ambition than that of making those around him happy.

In 1846, there was this entry in the diary: 'Three years of married life, dear Fanny! and you fairer than ever: each year an added grace, and a new charm in you, and in me new love and increase of affection.' A year later: 'Fanny was never more lovely, nor I more in love. All hail! O Tenth of May!' On the tenth anniversary of his engagement: 'A day always to be marked with a white stone!' Shortly after her death, in a hasty penciled note to her sister:

> I never looked at her without a thrill of pleasure. She never came into a room where I was, without my heart beating quicker, nor went out without my feeling that something of the light went with her.... That noble, loyal, spiritual nature always up-lifted and illuminated mine, and always will, to the end.

It cannot be gainsaid that Puritanism engendered certain unlovely by-products. In November, 1839, Longfellow noted:

> Walked to the Insane Hospital. Saw there several old ac-quaintances: Mr. Abbot, Mr. Paine, the former editor of the Portland Advertiser, Flagg, the artist, and Wolcot the anti-quary.

The illustrious Simrock, a gem in Germany's literary crown, was effectively damned in Longfellow's estimation because he threw summersaults at a picnic on the Drachenburg. Our poet, however, transcended the more rigid bonds of tradition:

> Rather cheerless is the aspect of our early history. The stern old puritanical character rises above the common level of life; it has a breezy air about its summits, but they are bleak and forbidding.

On December 25, 1856, he deplored the 'old Puritan feeling' which prevents Christmas from being a 'cheerful, hearty holiday.' He sincerely regretted, but did not 'suppress,' Charley's military passion: he even took him from Nahant to Boston, to get him a cap and belt. During a bleak spring, he 'heightened the color of his pale happiness' by reading French history; he hinted humorously at the old strictness in a letter to his father concerning the Lowell Lectures of 1840:

They have been delivered at the Odeon; which in days gone by was the Federal Street Theatre. Many who would not for the world venture to a play, have here something of the same excitement, without any of the sin.

It requires a born aristocrat to rise above instinctive impulses: a 'gentleman' Longfellow was. The older American type was pretty well submerged during the periods of immigration and frontier life, and has been well-nigh superseded, since the habit was formed of thinking of life in terms of business success, and of gentleness as emasculation. Mr. J. T. Adams holds that the pernicious type of unscrupulous business man began its detrimental development in New York. A highminded consideration for others, a generous wish to praise and recommend those who had not received recognition, a scrupulous reserve in regard to his own person and achievements — all these are eminently characteristic of this son of New England. Serene under depreciation and envy, even the scurrilous accusations of Poe failed to arouse resentment. When the latter, conscious of having charged Longfellow with flat plagiarism, wrote to gain his assistance in furthering *Graham's Magazine*, he indicated that he was 'not favorably known' — which can hardly be called an overstatement. Longfellow, in courteously refusing,[1] answered:

> You are mistaken.... All that I have read from your pen has inspired me with a high idea of your power; and I think you are destined to stand among the first romance-writers of the country.

After Poe's death, Longfellow wrote:

> I have always entertained a high appreciation of his powers as a prose writer and a poet.... The harshness of his criticisms I have never attributed to anything but the irritation of a sensitive nature chafed by some indefinite sense of wrong.

[1] He later became a regular contributor to this magazine.

[155]

Und hinter ihm, in wesenlosem Scheine,
Lag, was uns alle bändigt, das Gemeine!

Human sympathy, according to his gifted brother and biographer, was the first element in his nature. *The Challenge* shows clearly that the 'soft-stuffed repose' of Craigie House did not deafen him to the 'cold and darkness and hunger and despair' of the less-favored. *The Jewish Cemetery at Newport* proves that a New England Puritan could enter, with finest feeling, into the heart of an alien and despised group. He came to be recognized as 'the general superintendent of all the dilapidated and tumble-down foreigners who pass this way,' — and who were quite likely to reward his kindness by the sheerest insolence. How any man could be subjected to such a bombardment, without going mad, remains a problem. He made heroic efforts to bring Freiligrath with his entire family into his intimate circle — where it is conceivable that this pre-eminently 'German' group might have been regarded askance by the Brahminic caste of Cambridge. Notable was his affectionate care for the ill-starred Greene, intimate friend of his youth. He not only bought him a home in East Greenwich, but in 1870 added a windmill, which was moved, and attached as a library tower. At the age of seventy-three, Longfellow traveled to East Greenwich, to attend the wedding of his friend's daughter. When Greene had completely given out, he was made an inmate of Craigie House, where Longfellow ministered personally to his most intimate needs, and the lowliest duties on himself did lay. *Ultima Thule*, Longfellow's last volume (1880), was dedicated to him in a tender opening poem. Not all of the poet's friends were of the dependent class: he had a supreme gift of winning the affection which he most generously nourished; the roster of his intimates is a *Who's Who* of the times.

Longfellow was a mild 'liberal' in religion. He made a searching study of the 'foundations' by reading the Christian Fathers. As a Bowdoin undergraduate, he 'staged' a mannerly revolt against the rigid orthodoxy of the college. Much later, he praised Moncure D. Conway's rather radical sermon on 'Skeptics.' He had a kindly sympathy with Evangelicals and Catholics: 'there is much in the Catholic worship which I like.' In *Kavanagh* he speaks of 'that august faith.' None the less, the editor of the *North American Review* asked him to 'soften a little some passages which bear hard upon the peculiar opinions of the Catholics'; he could parody, with trenchant satire, abuses which had grown about the Holy Apostolic Faith. A regular church-goer, he was 'not ashamed to pray'; he believed in immortality, and an accounting for the deeds done in the body; his own work was conscientiously wrought in the spirit of that age when 'Art was still Religion':

> Take it, O Lord, and let it be
> As something I have wrought for Thee!

Er ist unser! The historic tradition which he upheld is America's best inheritance from the past. His writings and his life constitute a Work of Art of singular unity and beauty:

> — sein Leben
> Liegt faltenlos und leuchtend ausgebreitet,
> Kein dunkler Flecken blieb darin zurück.

APPENDIX A

LONGFELLOW'S GERMAN FRIENDS AND CORRESPONDENTS

THE following list contains the names of those Germans with whom the poet had more intimate converse:

Adler, Prof. G. J., a meritorious scholar, author of an important German dictionary, who lived in New York in very straitened circumstances. Much correspondence from 1848 to 1868.

Arnold, George, of Nuremberg. Translated L.'s poem on that city. Correspondence from 1862 to 1866, and interchange of books.

Beck, Professor Charles, German scholar who fled to the United States with Charles Follen, in 1824. Widely known as Professor of Latin in Harvard. Belonged to L.'s more intimate circle, and labored valiantly to bring Freiligrath and his family to America. Died March 19, 1866.

Böttger, Adolf, poet in Leipzig. In 1856 he wrote a very complimentary letter to L., and sent his own translations of *Hiawatha* and *Hyperion.*

Böttiger, Hofrat, Dresden. L. presented a letter of introduction from Washington Irving, on January 26, 1829. He offered L. the use of his library, and other facilities for study. L. borrowed Spanish books from his collection.

Elizabeth, Princess of Roumania. Sent L. her German poem, in seven stanzas, in 1876.

Elze, Dr. Karl, of Dessau. Editor of a collection of American Standard Authors. Correspondence, 1862 and 1868.

Follen, Prof. Charles (1796–1840), youthful singer of revolutionary songs in Germany; fled to America, 1824; first Professor of German Language and Literature at Harvard (1830–1835). Became a Unitarian minister. Recommended Bernard Rölker to L. as Instructor in German. On very friendly terms with L.

[159]

Freiligrath, Ferdinand (1810–1876), noted German poet, one of L.'s dearest friends. See Chapter VII.

Gall, Fräulein Louise von, brilliant member of Freiligrath's circle at St. Goar, 1842. Married Levin Schücking. L. wrote to her as late as 1852. See Chapter VII.

Gräter, a German in Boston, with whom L. had associations. Mentioned 1838. In 1841, L. gave him advice as to the translation of German stories.

Haardt, Dr., poet and man-of-letters, who made an unsuccessful attempt to establish himself in Boston. Had been a friend of Justinus Kerner. L. tried to form a class for his readings (1854), and helped him in various ways. Frequent caller at Craigie House. Died suddenly, February 29, 1856. 'A gentleman, and a proud one; and the misery of his last year had eaten his heart.' L. attended his funeral at Mount Auburn.

Hepp, family in Heidelberg, in whose charge L. placed Miss Clara Crowninshield in December, 1835. L. maintained a long German correspondence with the daughter, Julie.

Heuberger, Landrat H. C., L.'s first friend in Marienberg, 1842. Introduced L. to Freiligrath. Correspondence until 1876. See Chapter VII.

Hohenhausen, Elise, Baronin von, of Frankfurt a.d.Oder. Translated *The Golden Legend*, 1857. Correspondence, 1857 and 1867.

Hunold, B., Secretary of the National Museum at Innsbruck. Made a very popular translation of *Excelsior*. Honorific letter from him, 1859.

Julius, Dr. N. H., of Hamburg. Came to this country to study American affairs (left in 1836); published various volumes on the subject. Considerable correspondence, 1838–1852. In 1842, asked L. for *Hyperion*, and proposed to make the Germans acquainted with it. 1852 sent L. a German translation of *Evangeline*.

Keck, Dr. Carl, of Schloss Aistershaim, Austria. October, 1859, sent L. his translation of *The Golden Legend*, with letter.

APPENDIX A

Knortz, Karl, German-American writer and poet. Translated *Evangeline*, *Hiawatha*, and *Miles Standish*. Much correspondence, 1869–1877.

Kohl, Dr. J. G., of Bremen. State Librarian, geographer, and historian; brother of the Countess Baudissin. Large and frequent correspondence, and interchange of books, 1859–1877. He visited Cambridge in 1857, and was entertained by L. Published *Skizzen aus Nord-Amerika*, 1862. 'A very admirable, excellent man.'

Lieber, Dr. Francis (1800–1872), distinguished publicist and author. Came to United States in 1827. Professor at Columbia, S. C. (1835–1856), and in Columbia University, N. Y. (1857–1872). One of L.'s notable acquaintances. Much correspondence, and many personal contacts (1835–1872). 'A strong man, whose conversation sets your wheels all in motion.' He gave L. important introductions for Heidelberg, 1835.

Liszt, Franz (1811–1886), noted composer, Hungarian by birth; lived for many years in Weimar. Some association in Rome, 1869. He set to music the Introduction to *The Golden Legend*.

Mayer, Brantz, German-American of Baltimore, Md. During Goethe's life-time, American Consul in Weimar. Goethe presented him with a snuff-box. Much correspondence, 1852–1867. L. called on him in Baltimore.

Nielo, August Rudolf, of Braunschweig. In 1857, sends L. a German translation of his lyrics (Münster, 1857), and asks for an explanation of certain dark allusions. L. speaks of his translations as 'very cleverly done.' (Referred to as 'Nials' in *Life*.)

Perabeau, Charles. German musician, settled in the United States. Composed songs by L., and wrote him frequent German letters, from 1846. 'Ernst Perabo, the young musician' (*Life*, 3, 107), may have been a son?

Pfizer, Prof. Gustav (1807–1890), eminent man-of-letters, editor of the *Morgenblatt* in Stuttgart. Translated L.'s *Indian Hunter*; L. translated his *Der Junggeselle*, to his complete satisfaction. Wrote to L. in 1872. See Chapter VII. Having lost his own wife, he transl. L.'s *Footsteps of Angels*, 1872.

[161]

Ramm, Baron Jacques von, a German-speaking Russian, with an estate at Baltisport, in Esthonia. L's close friend and walking-companion in Heidelberg, 1836; well-versed in literature. The 'Baron' of *Hyperion*. Long letters from him in 1836 and 1839.

Raster, Hermann, editor of the *Abendpost*, New York. Correspondence in 1862.

Raumer, Friedrich von (1781–1873), historian. Interesting letter to L. (September 21, 1844), comparing European and American civilizations.

Robinson, Mrs. Edward (1797–1869), linguist and author. Before marriage, known by pen-name, 'Talvj' (Theresa Albertina Luise von Jakob). L. made her acquaintance at Dr. S. G. Howe's, June 11, 1848.

Rölker, Bernard, Instructor in Harvard, beginning September, 1838. One of L.'s best friends. See Chapter V.

Schele de Vere, Maximilian (Baron), born in Sweden, November 1, 1820. Studied in Berlin and Bonn (Ph.D., 1841), and entered Prussian military and diplomatic service. 1843, came to U. S. September, 1844, elected Professor of Modern Languages at the University of Virginia. Retired from active service, 1895. Died at Washington, D. C., May 10, 1898. Considerable correspondence.

Scherb, Emmanuel Vitalis, German-speaking immigrant from Basel. Introduced at Craigie House, 1848. Well-versed in literature; admired, consulted, and frequently entertained by L. Suggested subject of *New England Tragedies*. 1860, called to Charleston, S. C., as Universalist minister. (Adverse estimate in Ernest W. Longfellow's *Random Memories*.)

Schlickum, German painter, met L. at Rolandseck, July 25, 1842. Sent a painting to L. 1851, removed to Michigan.

Schurz, Carl (1829–1906), statesman and reformer. First call at Craigie House, April 19, 1859. 'He is a friend of Freiligrath; studied at Bonn, and, being a German patriot, has taken refuge in the far West. He is a keen-looking young man, and said to be a man of talent and influence.' 1872, called and stayed to dinner:

discussed Sumner's 'battle-flag resolution' (which later played so important a part in Schurz's eloquent tribute delivered after Sumner's death.)

Siedhof, Dr. Carl, educator. Conducted a boys' school in Massachusetts. Frequent intimate correspondence, beginning 1849. L. attended his silver wedding.

Simon, Carl Hermann, Leipzig. In 1872, received *The Divine Tragedy* from L. L. wrote him a long letter on March 12, 1874, expressing pleasure at Simon's translation of the *Tragedy*, and answering 35 questions as to the meaning of certain passages. 1876, Simon acknowledged receipt of L.'s *Works*. He translated and published L.'s *Sämtliche poetische Werke* (Leipzig). Sent L. his own poetical works, in 11 vols.

Simrock, Professor Karl, of the University of Bonn (1802–1876), poet and translator. Joined Freiligrath's 'Rhine-party' on July 25, 1842. L. called on him in Bonn on September 10, 1842. See Chapter VII. '42, sent L. his tr. of *Macbeth*.

Stolterfoth, Adelheid von, poetess and author in Freiligrath's circle, 1842. Her *Rheinische Lieder und Sagen* and *Rheinischer Sagen-Kreis* are in Craigie House. See Chapter VII.

Strodtmann, Adolf (1829–1879), Hamburg, editor of *Orion*; biographer of Heine. In 1863, wrote to L., soliciting a prose-article on American writers; also original poems.

Tellkampf, Johann Ludwig, professor in Union College. Versed in civil polity, French, Italian, and German. 1838–1839 was to pass the winter in Boston, and deliver lectures on German philosophy. December, 1839, was an entertaining guest at a convivial party given by Dr. Beck, which L. attended.

Thies, Louis, a friend and countryman of Dr. J. G. Kohl, of Bremen. He became curator of the collection of engravings given to Harvard by Frank Gray (about the beginning of 1858). Often mentioned by L. and Sumner. He married Clara Crowninshield. See Chapter IV.

Traub, Fräulein Fanny, Bremen. Wrote copiously to L., 1867–1876. L. wrote to her in June, 1877.

Tuckermann, Gen.-Lieut. a.D., Bonn. Corresponded with L. Translated a number of his lyric poems.

Voss, Hermann, nephew of the poet, J. H. Voss, living in Newark, N. J. Considerable correspondence, 1875–1877. In 1877, he sent L. autographs of Pfeffel and Voss.

Wesselhoeft, Dr., German physician residing in Cambridge. He had taken part in the student-demonstration at the Wartburg, 1817. Probably recommended the water-cure at Marienberg, 1842. Gave L. introductions to prominent Germans at the time of his third visit to Europe. Established a water-cure at Brattleboro, Vt., at which L. spent the summer of 1845.

Witte, Prof. Karl, Halle. Prominent Dante-scholar. Correspondence, 1867, 1872. L. sent him a large-paper copy of the translation of *The Divine Comedy* in 1872.

B

LONGFELLOW'S GERMAN STUDIES AND READING

THIS list does not include a catalogue of Mr. Longfellow's private library, which is preserved in Craigie House, Cambridge.

ABBREVIATIONS. Heid.: Heidelberg residence, extending from December 11, 1835, to August 27, 1836; Hyp.: *Hyperion*, published 1839; Ment.: mentioned; Tr.: translation; Publ.: published.

Ambraser Liederbuch. Two stanzas copied into notebook at Bowdoin, '33.

Annolied. Read in Heid.

Anonymous. The authorship of the following poems has not been established:
Forsaken ('Something the heart must have'). The first stanza was used as motto to Book Two of *Hyp.* In May, '48, L.

wrote: 'I thought of the German song,' and quoted the first
and last stanzas. Complete tr. first publ. '78.
The Happiest Land ('There sat one day in quiet'), publ. '39.
Song of the Rhine ('Forth rolled the Rhine-stream'), Cambr. Ed.
653.

Auerbach. 'Tom read us (in English) *The Professor's Wife*' (Feb.
6, '51). July 29, '51, L. read *Der Tolpatsch*, 'very clever, but not
equal to *The Professor's Wife.*'

Auersperg ('Anastatius Grün'). Read from him on Aug. 2, '36;
Dec. 12, '39; ment. Aug. 6, '42; Feb. 9, '48.

Becker, Nikolaus. June '42, refers to his 'single poem.' Read collected poems at Marienberg, '42; Oct. 1, '45, notes B.'s death in
diary: 'not a great poet, but had the felicity to touch the hearts
of his countrymen in a song of the Rhine.'

Binzer, Frau von (Cologne). Read her story, *Die Verlobung*, Aug.
27, '42.

Börne. Jan. '48, his *Schriften* received.

Brant. *Narrenschiff* carefully studied in Heid. Ment. in *Hyp.* and
in the *Cobbler of Hagenau*, '72.

Brentano, Bettina. Her 'correspondence with Goethe' referred
to in *Hyp.*

Brentano, Clemens. May 28, '38, Dr. Julius, of Hamburg, recom-
mends to L. *Gockel, Hinkel und Gakeleia*, as 'on the whole the
most remarkable German poetical publication during the last 20
years.' (See also *Volkslieder.*)

Bürger. A stanza from *Lenore*, tr. in *Outre-Mer*, '33. Two lines
from same poem quoted (in the original) in the *Blank Book of a
Country Schoolmaster*,' 34. In Heid., L. read B.'s *Life* and some
of his ballads; the *High Song of the Only One* he called 'a masterpiece of harmony.' '41, quotes a line from *Lenore*; '52, mentions
Scott's version of this ballad. '61, Freiligrath sent him the
'quaint first edition' of *Prinzessin Europa* (1777).

Carové. L. bought his *Moosblüten* (with plates after Runge) in
Heid. L.'s *Flowers*, written '37, speaks of 'One who dwelleth by

the castled Rhine,' who had called flowers the 'stars of earth.' This allusion, which mystified even Freiligrath, is from *Das Märchen ohne Ende*. It occurs also in *Hyp*.

Chamisso. *Peter Schlemihl* read in Heidelberg.

Claudius. His *Song of Rhine Wine* called 'one of the best' in *Hyp*. July 13, '39, mentioning an article on C., L. tr. a stanza from the *Happy Peasant*. '40, refers to a tr. of the *Song of Rhine Wine*.

Dach. L.'s tr. of *Ännchen von Tharau* and *Selig sind, die in dem Herrn sterben*, publ. '45.

Dingelstedt. '42, read *Lieder eines kosmopolitischen Nachtwächters*: 'vigorous and novel.'

Eberhard. '42, read *Hanchen und die Küchlein*; this poem also ment. '54. '73 (*Tales*), E. is referred to among the 'humble German bards.'

Eckermann. *Gespräche mit Goethe* read in Heid. Referred to in *Hyp*. Also read, '72.

Eichhorn. *Kulturgeschichte* and *Literaturgeschichte* acquired during professorship at Bowdoin, '29–'34.

Engel, J. J. Subject of special lecture at Harvard ('37 or '38), with special ment. of *Lorenz Stark, Der Philosoph für die Welt* and *Fürstenspiegel*.

Eschenburg. Cited in L.'s Harvard lecture on History of the German Language and Literature, '37 or '38.

Fichte. *Destiny of Man* ment. in *Hyp*. '46, L. read, with his wife, F.'s *Life*, by Smith; also the lectures on *The Nature of the Scholar* (see comment in Ch. VIII). The following June, L. and Sumner read together some chapters of the *Destiny*: 'F. believes the doctrine of necessity, — a pious, Christian fatalism.'

Flemming, Paul (XVII Cent.). Ment. in *Hyp*.

Flögel. *Geschichte der komischen Literatur* read in Heid.

Fouqué. *Undine* read in Heid. In '47, L. compares it with Milton's *Comus*.

Freiligrath. L. knew all his works.

Frey (   ). Poems read in Heidelberg.

Gall, Louise von (Frau Schücking). L. read her stories and poems in Marienberg, '42. See Ch. VII.

Geibel. Poems read at Marienberg, '42. (Name printed 'Geisel' in *Life*, I, 431.)

Gellert. L. bought complete Works at Bowdoin, about '33.

Gervinus. Cited as literary authority in Harvard lectures, '37 or '38.

Gleim. Anecdote of in *Hyp.*; quoted in Harvard lectures, '37 or '38.

Goethe. Throughout life, G. claimed a chief and ever-growing interest. A detailed discussion is made unnecessary since the appearance of O. W. Long's *Goethe and Longfellow*, in the *Germanic Review*, VII, 145–175. A forthcoming valuable study on the same subject by H. A. Pochmann (Yale Memorial volumes on *Goethe and America*; in preparation) is also announced. The only indications of study while in Göttingen, '29, are a five-line quotation from *Iphigenie*, and a sketch of himself, drawn by L., shown reading a volume of G. He doubtless became well oriented in the subject during his Bowdoin-professorship, '29–'34. *Outre-Mer*, '33, has one quotation from *Werther*, two from *Faust*. At Heid., intensive study began. *Hyp.*, having as its chief thesis, 'the cure of a morbid mind,' is related to *Werther* and *Wilhelm Meister*. Chapter Eight of the Second Book (originally entitled 'Old Humbug') was an attempt to give American readers an impression of G.'s totality. The First Part of *Faust* was drawn upon for six citations or allusions, the Second Part for two. Use is also made of *Iphigenie, Die Wahlverwandtschaften* ('that monstrous book'), and *Dichtung und Wahrheit*. (L.'s opinion of *Die Wahlverwandtschaften* did not change in later years. On July 27, 1851, there is the [unpublished] entry in his diary: 'Rölker dined with us; and read to me parts of his translation of Göthe's *Elective Affinities*. It is a strange thing altogether; and will smell offensively in this climate, whatever it may do in Germany. "Schöne Natur! du bist gar zu natürlich!" It is all well enough to translate the book if he likes it; but he had better let alone publishing it'). Four lyrics are introduced, including a tr. of *Über allen Gipfeln* (much inferior to that of '70) and the first stanza of *Wer nie sein Brot.*

Later allusions to Goethe (up to '80) are too numerous to recount. There is direct evidence of study of the lyric poems, *Werther, Faust, Egmont, Die Geschwister, Iphigenie, Wilhelm Meister, Hermann und Dorothea, Reineke Fuchs, Campagne in Frankreich, Italienische Reise, Die Wahlverwandtschaften, Dichtung und Wahrheit, Tag- und Jahreshefte, Briefe,* and *Gespräche.* L. publ. tr. of only 2 of G.'s lyrics. G. (especially *Faust*) had a leading place in L.'s lectures until the end of his professorship, '54 (cf. Ch. V). The statuette of G., bought in Heid., stood always (and still stands) on L.'s working-desk.

Gostwick. His *German Literature* read in '48.

Gottfried von Strassburg. '72, allusion to 'black sails,' from *Tristan und Isolde.*

Grillparzer. L. accidentally met him in the diligence bound for Salzburg, '36. '55, read the *Ahnfrau:* 'extremely effective.'

Grimm, Herman. *Michael Angelo* read in '42: 'most interesting and charmingly written.'

Grimm, Jakob. *Deutsche Grammatik* (3 vols.) procured and studied in Heid.

Gutzkow. Studied, '42; his *Börne* received, '48.

Hackländer. H. sent L. his *Vier Könige,* by way of Freiligrath, '42; on Sept. 6, L. read *Bilder von dem Soldatenleben.*

Hagen, August, '52, Mrs. Longfellow read aloud *Norica, or Tales of Nuremberg.*

Hagen, von der. Cited in lecture on Hist. of Ger. Lit., '37 or '38.

Hahn-Hahn, Ida von. '46, L. tr. a stanza from her *Lass, O Herr!* (*Life,* II, 32); '47, read her novel, *Ulrich.*

Hartmann von Aue. Used as basis of *The Golden Legend,* '39–'51.

Hauff. '52, read *Bettlerin des Pont-des-Arts.*

Hebel. His Alemannic poems read in Heid. H. is cited as a 'humble German bard' in *Tales*, '73.

Hedge, F. H. '71, *Prose Writers of Germany* read.

Heine. A page transcribed in notebook, Göttingen, '29. *Romantische Schule* read in Heid. '37, certain volumes borrowed from Miss Mary Appleton, with request for all (p. 50); estimate of H. in same letter. In lecture on 'German Tales and Traditions' ('38?), a long passage tr. from the *Harzreise* (So stillstehend... hinter'm Ofen). H.'s tribute to Goethe (from *Romantische Schule*) in Harvard lecture and *Hyp*. Article on H., '42, see p. 87). '43, tr. 'The Sea hath its Pearls'; estimate of *Buch der Lieder*, see p. 111. '46, '48, possible influence of H. on L.'s *Twilight* and *Fire of Driftwood*. '48, ment.; *Atta Troll* received from importer. '51, 'Read H.'s *Deutschland*, a sneering, sacastic, in parts indecent, Poem. H. is a true lyric poet; one of best Germany has produced.' The allusion to the 'boy of Bacharach,' in *The Golden Legend*, may derive from H.'s *Rabbi*. '53, reading from *Salon*: 'very clever and diabolical.' '54, 'Scherb read Heine's *Aveux d'un Poete* — witty and wicked as ever, though the writer is paralytic, and has been bed-ridden for five years.' '59, read *Lutetia*; '71, Strodtmann's *Life of H.* '79, much interested in Zendrini's Italian tr. of H.'s poems.

Heldenbuch. L. secured a good edition while at Bowdoin, cir. '33. Referred to in *Hyp*. '44, *Hugdietrich* and *Wolfdietrich* read.

Herder. L. obtained complete works (44 vols.) at Bowdoin, cir. '33. Read H. 'under the trees' with Baron von Ramm in Heid. (See *Volkslieder*.)

Herwegh. Poems read, '42: 'spirited, and mostly political... a young poet who writes in the vigorous style of the new school.' Ment. '48.

Hoffmann, E. T. A. '36, copiously read in Heid. Jan. 19: 'am getting out of patience with H. These tales of horror are entirely repugnant.' H.'s life and writings fully treated in lectures at Harvard, summer-course, '38. Same year, H.'s *Nussknacker* and *Serapionsbrüder* ordered from Germany. Much lecture-material incorporated into *Hyp.*, where is also a long tr. of

Kreisler's Musical Sufferings. Serapionsbrüder referred to, '41.
L. read *Olivier Brusson* in '47; refers to *Kater Murr*, '54.

Hoffmann von Fallersleben. At Schaffhausen, '36, read chapter on
H. v. F.: 'capital.' Ment. '48.

Hölty. Read in Heid. In diary of Feb. 5, '36, is a translation of two
stanzas of H.'s *Mailied:*

> Red and green is the meadow,
> Blue and golden the aether,
> Clear and silver the streamlet,
> Cool and shady the birchen wood.

> Herd-bells chime in the valley,
> Lambkins bleat by the brooklet,
> And the flute of the shepherd
> Wakes the slumbrous twilight grove.

Immermann. Poems and prose works read, '42: 'full of fancy; and
many of them are delicate and beautiful.' Aug. '42, Freiligrath
sends L. his book on I.

Jordan, Wilhelm. L. heard him recite from his own *Nibelungenlied*
in Boston, '72.

Kant. '53, read De Quincey's *Last days of K.* '71, read, in tr., K.'s
essay on the origin of man.

Keller, Georg Victor. '36, read his *Stunden der Andacht* (6 vols.).

Kerner. His *Saw-Mill* cited in *Kavanagh*, '49. (K. tr. L.'s *Walter
von der Vogelweid.*)

Kirchenlied. '33, tr. a stanza of J. Heermann's *Herzliebster Jesu.*
'42, L. orders a *Choralbuch* from Coblenz.

Klopstock. L. secured complete works in Bowdoin, cir. '33. Read
in Heid.

König, H. '42, read *Wilhelms Dichten und Trachten.*

Kopisch. L. used his *Volkstümliche Poesien aus allen Mundarten
Italiens* in writing *The Golden Legend.*

Körner, C. G. '72, read his correspondence with Schiller.

Körner, Theodor. Tr. of certain of his poems owned by L.'s wife, '31. Complete works acquired at Bowdoin, cir. '33. A tr. of his *Good Night,* in *The Token* for '35, signed 'L.', is doubtless by Longfellow. '43, *Life and Poems of K.* were bought. *The Golden Legend,* '51, contains the phrase, 'With lyre and sword.'

Lenau. Studied, '42; ment. '48.

Lessing. In Heid. read *Emilia Galotti* (comment, see p. 40); *Wie die Alten den Tod gebildet:* 'written with great clearness and acuteness,' and *Nathan der Weise:* 'I think highly of it; though it is not a masterpiece, and I do not like the way in which it closes. The story of the three rings...is beautiful, and as good as a sermon'; on May 8, he saw *Nathan* performed at Mannheim. Lessing's idea as to the ancient representation of Death is incorporated into *Hyp.* A German musician, who had composed Lessing's convivial *Der Tod,* asked L. for an English tr. in '47: 'I am not eager to plunge into the bacchanalian strain' (he had just completed *Evangeline*!). '59, *Emilia Galotti* was re-read: 'Very tragic, but dramatically of great power. The subject is not pleasant.'

Logau. Effective tr. of twelve *Sinngedichte,* publ. '45.

Ludwigslied. Read in Heidelberg.

Luther. One page tr. in Göttingen notebook, '29. Tr. of two lines of *Ein' feste Burg* in *Hyp.* L. drew the materials for the Interlude, *Martin Luther* (in *Christus*) from Luther's *Memoirs.* This Interlude includes a full tr. of *Ein' feste Burg.*

Mahlmann. The pleasing tr. of *Allah* (undated: from *Benno*) makes the last tr. in the Cambridge Edition.

Mailáth. *Altdeutsche Gedichte* furnished the text of *Der arme Heinrich;* also the story of the monk Felix, in *The Golden Legend,* '51.

Matthison. Formed subject of one of L.'s first Harvard lectures, '37 (see p. 53). Discussion of M.'s poetry in *Hyp.,* with tr. of one stanza from *Die Sterbende.* A statement in *Hyp.* as to 'the poet,' who 'has in his books the ruins of an antique world, his Apollo and Transfiguration,' is manifestly derived from M.'s *Kinderjahre:*

Da floss mir keine Zähre...
Verklärung, Belvidere
Und Kapitol zu schauen.

My Lost Youth, '55, has much kinship with the same poem.

Meistersinger. L. early acquired Grimm's *Über den altdeutschen Meistergesang.* In *Hyp.* and *Nuremberg* ('44) he makes fun of their peculiarities. Also ment. in *Cobbler of Hagenau,* '72.

Menzel. M.'s attack on Goethe is ment. in *Hyp.* In the same year, Felton discussed with L. his tr. of M.'s *History of German Literature.* L.'s review of this tr. was refused by Cogswell in '40, but publ. in the *New World.*

Minnesinger. Ment. in Rotterdam, '35, as inspiring Uhland's verse. Read a number in Heid. Ofterdingen, Frauenlob, Vogelweide, Toggenburg, and Hohenfels ment. in *Hyp.* '71, tried to secure printing of Kroeger's *Specimens,* in Cambridge. Ment. of Frauenlob in letter of '73. Allusions in *Walter von der Vogelweid,* '45, and *Herons of Elmwood,* '78.

Mosen. Tr. of *Das Steinbild am Dome* and *Der Kreuzschnabel,* '55. *Victor Galbraith,* '55, resembles *Andreas Hofer.*

Müller, Wilhelm. L. first introduced him to English readers. Tr. *Wohin?,* Feb. 1, '37 (included in *Hyp*: also last stanza of *Abendreihn*). Tr. of *Schiff und Vogel,* publ. '39. '46: 'Why does no one translate Müller's "Guten Abend, lieber Mondenschein"?' The story of Fastrada (*Golden Legend,* '51) may have been derived from M.'s *Saga vom Frankfurter See.* L. used M.'s *Dichter des XVII. Jahrhunderts* in tr. from Dach and Logau.

Nibelungenlied. L. secured a good edition at Bowdoin, cir. '33. Ment. among his Heid. studies in *Hyp.,* where also occurs the passage: 'all his wounds began to bleed afresh, like those of the murdered man when the murderer approaches.' Read from it in '42: 'quaint and vigorous; with a kind of Homeric simplicity.' '44 (and '72) read from Weber's treatise: 'Strange old poem! with great power in delineations of character, and many fine descriptions.' 'Bought an elegant copy,' '42, to present to Felton. '72, hears W. Jordan recite his version.

Novalis. Read *H. von Ofterdingen* with Miss Crowninshield in Heid.: 'Wild and singular... strangely beautiful thoughts peep out.' Quotation from in *Hyp.*

Opitz. Tr. of *The Stars* (undated) in Cambridge Ed., 654.

Pfinzing. '44, referred to in *Nuremberg,* and in letter to Freiligrath.

Pfizer. Tr. of *Der Junggesell* ('Two Locks of Hair'), '41. P. tr. L.'s *Indian Hunter.* In '72, after the loss of his own wife, he also tr. L.'s *Footsteps of Angels.*

Platen. Ment. '48. '70, tr. *Mut und Unmut* ('Remorse'). '72, recited same, in German, to Mrs. Fields.

Postl. See Sealsfield.

Puschmann. Used for Poem, *Nuremberg,* '44, and discussed in letter to Freiligrath, same year.

Richter ('Jean Paul'). See Deiml's dissertation: *Der Einfluss von Jean Paul auf L.'s Prosastil.* Tr. from R. were found in Mary L.'s copy of *The Literary Gem,* '31. 'The German moralist,' in *Outre-Mer,* '33, identified as R. by Campbell. *The Little Man in Gosling Green,* '34, shows traces of R.'s style. In Heid. read *Flegeljahre, Titan,* and *Campanertal,* and discussed the last with Baron von Ramm. Apr. 18, '36, in diary: 'Jean Paul runs into so many foolish extravagances in his style, that I get out of humor with him.' '37, calls R. 'the most magnificent of the German prose writers,' and quotes from *Quintus Fixlein.* '37, quotes him to Hawthorne. Largely stressed in Harvard lectures, from Spring of '37, on. In *Hyp.,* Ch. I, Book i, 'The Only One,' is devoted to him, with much material from diary and Harvard lectures. '40, lectured on him in New York. '41, cites *Leben Fibels.* '44 (and '46), Mrs. Longfellow read him *Die Flegeljahre:* 'How fine are the figures!' '48, received new tr. of *Levana,* which 'filled the room with a kind of intellectual aroma.' '48, with wife, read *Campanertal.* '63, read Brooks' tr. of *Titan:* 'splendid book, wild and wonderful.' '64, quotes R.

Rosenkranz. '36, read his *Geschichte der Poesie:* passage from this introduced into *Hyp.*

Sachs. Alluded to in *Hyp., Nuremberg* ('44) and *Tales*, '72.

Salis-Seewis. The *Silent Land* (in *Hyp.*, where also a characterization of the 'morbid' poet) was tr. in Heid., Feb. 6, '36.

Sallet, Friedrich von. Ment. among 'political poets,' '48.

Saxon Chronicles. Studied in Heid., ment. in *Hyp.*

Schefer, Leopold. '48, read S.'s *Albrecht Dürer*: 'admirable art-novel.'

Scheible. '48, *Kloster* received from importer.

Schelling. L. tr. *Dante from a Philosophical Point of View*, '46: 'deep, — obscure, rather'; sent to *Graham's Magazine*, '50.

Schenkendorf. *Song of the Rhine* ment. as 'one of the best' in *Hyp.*

Schiller. June, '35, read Carlyle's *Life*: 'noble delineation of that great and good man'; on river-trip to Richmond remarked: 'the whole scene one of enchantment, like that one the Brenta, described in Schiller's *Geisterseher*.' Discussed with Mrs. Carlyle the relative merits of Goethe and S.; soon after arrival in Heid., Dec. '35, argues with Frl. Hepp, in German, on the same subject. In Holland, read S.'s lyrics with Miss Crowninshield. In Heid.: *Don Carlos* (attended a lecture by Reichlin-Meldegg on this drama), *Dreissigjähriger Krieg, Wallenstein* (of *Piccolomini*: 'language rich, the characters well developed, but, as in *Don Carlos*, a want of movement; action is overloaded with words'; of *Wallenstein's Tod*: 'fine — in parts magnificent; closing with scenes of painful interest'). *Hyp.* contains two short tr. from *Wallenstein*. '41, L. heard *The Bell* at the Odeon in Boston, with Ramberg's music. '43, the scene between Victorian and Preciosa, in *The Spanish Student*, somewhat resembles a situation in *Kabale und Liebe*. '44, L. writes into his diary a (deplorable) tr. of Thekla's song. '46, *Pegasus in Pound* is much like S.'s *Pegasus im Joche*. '47, quotes a line from *Teilung der Erde* in letter to Freiligrath; same year, makes interesting variants on S.'s distich on elegiac meter. '48, read *Tell*. *Building of the Ship* ('49), *Hanging of the Crane* ('74), and *Kéramos* ('78) suggests S.'s *Bell* in structure. '52 (also '53), quotes from *Ritter Toggenburg*; also from *Wallenstein*. '53, quotes from *Teilung der*

Erde. '55, quotes from *Bell.* '59, attends great Schiller-Festival in Boston. Tr. *Columbus* for Sumner (undated). '72, re-reads *Don Carlos* (see p. 134); also correspondence with Körner (p. 133). '75, quotes from *Wallen tein.* '79, refers to *Ring von Polykrates.* '81, elegiac verses suggest those of Goethe and S.

Schlegel, A. W. von. In *Outre-Mer,* '33, quotation from *Vorlesungen über die schöne Literatur.* L. called on him in Bonn, Dec. 7, 1835. '72, read *Lectures on Dramatic Literature.*

Schlegel, Fr. v. '72 read S.'s *Lectures on the History of Literature.*

Schleiermacher. '35, read his *Letters on Lucinde.*

Schreiber. Transl. his *An die Glocke,* on June 6, '36; publ. in *Hyp.*: 'Bell, thou soundest merrily.'

Schröter. Read S.'s tr. of *Finnische Runen* (important for *Hiawatha*) on June 27, '42; referred to in letters to Freiligrath, '43 and '55.

Schubert. *Geschichte der Seele* read in Heid. Referred to in *Hyp.*

Sealsfield (Postl.). '44, read *American Sketches*; '47, *Cabin Book* (tr. by Mersch): 'delicious description of natural scenery.' '47: 'In the evening we read our favorite Sealsfield. Description of the South West very striking; the passage through a cypress-swamp terrible.'

Simrock. Read *Rheinsagen,* '42.

Stockmann. *Wie sie so sanft ruhn* was tr. in '38: 'purely verbal.'

Stolberg, Chr. and Fr. Poems read in Heidelberg. Owned complete works in 20 vols.

Stolterfoth. Her writings sent to L. by Freiligrath on Aug. 30, '42. See Chapter VII.

Studentenlieder. A number were transcribed in the *Old Dominion Zeitung,* '29. In Göttingen diary, a stanza from *Die Schöne Nachbarin* (see p. 18). *Was kommt dort,* tr., in full, in *Hyp.* L. often sang German student-songs in Cambridge, with his friends Rölker and Beck.

Tieck. Read much in Heid. In *Hyp.*: 'He and Uhland are the best living poets of Germany.' '38, read *Phantasien über die Kunst.* T. stressed in Harvard lectures, '38. '40, read *Franz Sternbald,* 'a Claude Lorraine atmosphere about the book which is delightful.' '41, advises against tr. of T.'s *Tales.* '53: 'Rölker read to me *Der blonde Eckert.*'

Tiedge. *Urania* discussed (unfavorably) in *Hyp.* L.'s tr. of *Die Welle* publ. '39.

Uhland. '35, read poems in Rotterdam. '36, fails to find U. in Stuttgart; reads him in Switzerland: tr. of *Castle by the Sea,* with help of Miss Fanny Appleton. *Hyp.* contains this, also tr. of *Der schwarze Ritter,* and *Die Überfahrt* (latter not by L.); ment. of *Der Tod eines Landgeistlichen.* L.'s tr. of *Das Glück von Edenhall,* '41. '48, ment. receipt of book with sketch of U. '59, recalls *Der Tod eines Landgeistlichen.* '72, receives a comprehensive U. –catalogue, and considers making purchases.

Varnhagen von Ense. On June 2, '63, L. expresses interest in his *Memoirs* and *Diary.*

Volksbücher. '35, read Low-German *Reynke de Vos,* in Rotterdam (see p. 35); ment. in *Cobbler of Hagenau,* '72. Eulenspiegel ment. in *Hyp.,* and *Cobbler of Hagenau,* '72. Read Görres' *Volksbücher* in Heid. '42, read 'the popular tale of St. Genevieve.' '48, acquired Scheible's *Kloster.*

Volkslieder. Of especial interest to L. '29, copied from *Nachtwächterlied.* '36, copied into diary the folk-songs:

> Sag' einmal, sag' einmal,
> Vöglein, wo ziehst du hin?, etc.;

and

> Alles sehen und nichts sprechen, etc.

Sept. '36, *Kömmt a Vogel,* etc. (see p. 47). L. bought the First Edition of the *Wunderhorn* in Heid. (see p. 40): in *Hyp.* Flemming knows the *Wunderhorn* 'almost by heart'; the last stanza of *Die Schlacht bei Murten* (tr. in *Hyp.*) is from this source. Herder's *Volkslieder* is the source of the Greenland funeral-song ment. in *Hyp*. (In *Kavanagh*, '49: 'thought of Lapland sledges, and the song of Kulnasatz'; also the 'Lapland Song' of *My Lost Youth* is from this source.)

Erlach's *Volkslieder* were acquired in Heid., and were repeatedly quoted. 'Take Care!' (*Hyp*.) was derived from this (also *Silent Love*, tr. '45, which is the first stanza of Erlach's *Gute Lehre*). *Hyp*. contains, also, 'Oh, how the drum,' and the 'cuckoo'-song (taken down in L.'s diary, May 25, '36). Other *Volkslieder* are ment. in diaries. '42, L. ordered Wedemann's *Volkslieder* from Coblenz. L.'s tr. of *O Tannenbaum* publ. '45. Ziska und Schottky's collection cited in lectures, '37 or '38. L. owned Uhland's *Volkslieder* and Meinert's *Alte teutsche Volkslieder*.

Volksmärchen. Read Grimm's and Musäus *V*. in Heid.

Voss. '29, copied a line from *Luise* into Göttingen notebook. '33, a page of extracts from same at Bowdoin. *Hyp*. refers to his 'idyls.' '54, *Luise* ment. '63, V. is cited as 'a humble German bard, (in *Tales*). '76, read V.'s *Briefe*.

Wackernagel. *Altdeutsches Lesebuch* studied in Heid. Cited in early Harvard lectures.

Walther von der Vogelweide. Ment. in *Hyp*. Poem on subject, '45; character in *Golden Legend*, '51.

Weber. *Teutonic Metrical Romances* bought in Copenhagen, '35: Re-read in '71.

Werner. His *Schicksalsdramen* ment. in *Hyp*.

Wheaton. *Address on German Literature*, read in '47.

Wieland. Notebook, '33, copies a page concerning W.'s poetry. '34, read one of his *Psalms*. '38, quotes from *Briefe an einen jungen Dichter*. Anecdote of ('the great I of Osmannstadt'), quoted in *Hyp*.; where also: 'like Hüon of Bordeaux and Scherasmin on their way to Babylon,' and 'Angulaffer's castle in *Oberon*.' '39, considers *Oberon* inferior to *Faery Queen*.

Wolff, O. L. B. '42, read and copied *Der gute George Campbell*.

Zedlitz. *Die nächtliche Heerschau* read in Heid. Ment. '42.

Zimmermann. *Bauernkrieg* gotten in '48.

Zschokke. *Tales* referred to, '41. '46, reads *The Sleepwalker*, in Godwin's tr., i.e.: *Die Verklärungen*.

BIBLIOGRAPHY

IN THIS list no attempt is made to include the enormous mass of Longfellow-literature. The titles which follow have a special relation to the present work.

Samuel Longfellow: *Life of Henry Wadsworth Longfellow.* Three volumes, Boston, 1891. Houghton, Mifflin and Company.
This admirable work, characterized by objectivity, fulness, accuracy, and urbanity, remains the chief source of information concerning the poet. Cited as *Life.*

Oskar Thiergen: *Longfellow und seine Beziehungen zur deutschen Literatur. Zeitschrift für den deutschen Unterricht,* VI, 267 (1892).
J. P. Worden: *Über Longfellow's Beziehungen zur deutschen Litteratur.* Dissertation, Halle, 1900.
T. M. Campbell: *Longfellows Wechselbeziehungen zu der deutschen Literatur.* Dissertation, Leipzig, 1907.
Alex. Baumgartner, S.J.: *Longfellows Dichtungen.* Freiburg i. Br., 1887.
Charles Follen: *Works and Memoir.* Boston, 1841.
T. W. Higginson: *Henry Wadsworth Longfellow.* Boston, 1902.
Edward E. Hale, Jr.: *Life and Letters of Edward Everett Hale.* Boston, 1917.
Ernest W. Longfellow: *Random Memories.* Boston, 1922.
Henrietta Dana Skinner: *An Echo from Parnassus.* New York, 1928.
W. A. Chamberlin: *Longfellow's Attitude toward Goethe. Modern Philology,* XVI, 1–20 (1918).
O. W. Long: *Goethe and Longfellow. Germanic Review,* VII, 145–175 (1932). A fundamental survey, based on original manuscripts. Extends its scope to the consideration of other authors than Goethe.
H. A. Pochmann: *Goethe and Longfellow.* Yale Goethe Memorial Volumes (in preparation).
Otto Deiml: *Der Einfluss von Jean Paul auf Longfellows Prosastil.* Dissertation, Erlangen, 1927.

[179]

BIBLIOGRAPHY

Maria Appelmann: *H. W. Longfellow's Beziehungen zu Ferdinand Freiligrath.* Dissertation, Münster i. W., 1915.

Käthe Freiligrath-Kroeker: *Ein Rhein-Idyll.* Deutsche Revue, April, 1901.

Luise Wiens: *Ungedrucktes von Ferdinand Freiligrath.* Deutsche Rundschau, CXLV, 143 (1910).

E. G. Gudde: *Freiligraths Entwicklung als politischer Dichter.* Berlin, 1922.

Festreden bei der Erinnerungsfeier an Everett, Bancroft, Longfellow und Motley. Göttingen, 1890.

J. T. Hatfield: *Longfellow's 'Lapland Song.'* Publications of the Modern Language Association of America, XLV, 1188.

J T. Hatfield: *An Unknown Prose Tale by Longfellow.* American Literature, April, 1931.

J. T. Hatfield: *The Longfellow-Freiligrath Correspondence.* Publications of the Modern Language Association of America, December, 1933.

INDEX

INDEX OF PERSONS

This index does not include the material in the two Appendices, where personal names are also listed in alphabetical order.

[183]

INDEX

INDEX

INDEX

INDEX